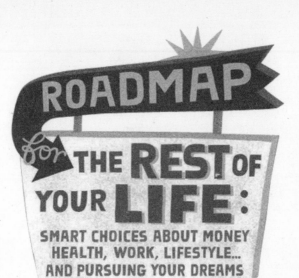

ROADMAP for THE REST OF YOUR LIFE:

SMART CHOICES ABOUT MONEY
HEALTH, WORK, LIFESTYLE...
AND PURSUING YOUR DREAMS

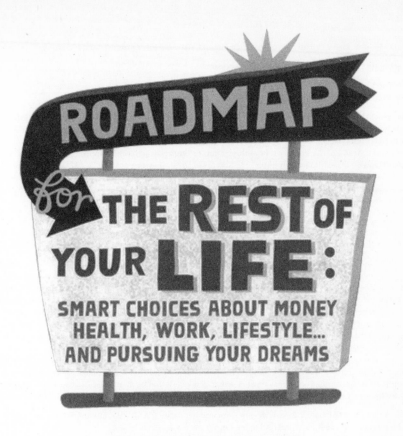

ROADMAP
for THE REST OF YOUR LIFE:
SMART CHOICES ABOUT MONEY
HEALTH, WORK, LIFESTYLE...
AND PURSUING YOUR DREAMS

BART ASTOR

WILEY

Published by John Wiley & Sons, Inc., Hoboken, New Jersey.
Published simultaneously in Canada.

Library of Congress Cataloging-in-Publication Data:

Astor, Bart.
    Roadmap for the rest of your life : smart choices about money health, work, lifestyle . . . and pursuing
your dreams / Bart Astor.
      pages   cm
    Subtitle should read:
    Includes index.
    ISBN 978-1-118-40112-5 (pbk.); ISBN 978-1-118-79575-9 (ebk); ISBN 978-1-118-49568-1 (ebk);
    ISBN 978-1-118-49572-8 (ebk)
      1. Retirement–Planning.   2. Older people–Finance, Personal.   3. Aging–Social aspects.
4. Lifestyles.   I. Title.
HQ1062.A78   2013
332.024'014–dc23
                                                  2012051174

Printed in the United States of America
10 9 8 7 6 5 4 3 2 1

To Kathie, the North Star on my roadmap

Contents

Contents

Foreword

When you imagine the rest of your life after 50, do you see a boat, a sports car, a summer home, cruising the Amazon or climbing Kilimanjaro, or finding a quiet corner in your backyard, or a patch of thatched cottage in the Caribbean, to curl up and write your memoir?

Have you also factored in the cost of a grown child's wedding, the travel costs to see your scattered children and grandkids, and the grandbaby who turns four before you know it and will need about $10,000 for a good prekindergarten? The question is not just how long you want to work, but how long you need to work. And I mean need not just in the sense of financial need, but the psychological need to have colleagues to talk to, phone calls to return, and the feeling of being valued.

We have learned a great deal about how to set goals for our First Adulthood and how to roll with the punches when we hit a rough passage. But our Second Adulthood, when we really have grown up, presents a much less linear roadmap. There are no fixed entrances or exits, and there is a lot of sand in which it is easy to bury our heads. Many of us over 50 turn into ostriches. We may be totally rational when we look at a profit-and-loss statement in business. But we don't like to look at our personal assets and project the changes in profit when we're no longer working full tilt, or the possibility that digitalization will make our former job obsolete, or the cost of caring for Dad when Mom dies. We don't really want to look at what's right in front of us: another 30, 40, even possibly 50 years of life to be financed and filled with meaningful activities and replenished relationships.

Bart Astor's friendly, experience-based book focuses on all that and is surprisingly readable. It is a book for those of us who don't want to be victims.

Foreword

I'm guilty of being an ostrich. When I finally did force myself to sit down with Astor's manuscript, I found myself returning to the central question facing us as we move into our Second Adulthood: What are our goals for this stage in our lives? There really are no more "shoulds." Our parents and mentors and bosses don't have much to say about our choices at this stage. A spouse, if we have one, might be one of the Worried Well—people who anticipate the worst, save for a rainy day, and buy the most expensive long-term care insurance. They may even prepay for pet burial. Those people will never run out of money. I'm not one of them.

Financial planners tell me there are many more ostriches than Worried Well. Even a very affluent person, let's say a successful single woman who figures she will cut back to half-time work at 66 and retire completely at 70, may think assets worth a million dollars plus her house are enough to last the rest of her life. But once she cuts her income in half by working part-time, and the cost of living goes up 5 percent a year, and she has to pay taxes on the money she takes out of her individual retirement account (IRA), and she continues with the same lifestyle and spending habits like buying $500 boots, and she wants to pay for her grandson to go to medical school, she may run out of money before she's 80. Then the staggering cost of long-term care for chronic illness or disability kicks in and she's stunned, like so many people, that Medicare does not pay for long-term care.

I found Astor's 11 chapters very helpful in breaking down the right questions into manageable steps, with capsule life stories and helpful tips. He starts us off by defining how much activity we can manage. That's smart. Setting the goal of opening an independent bookstore might sound idyllic, but not if we aren't fit enough to haul around a lot of very heavy books. How about creating a commercial book-swapping website instead? Or going into business with a son or daughter who can do the heavy lifting while you develop the strategic plans for engaging a following?

Especially thoughtful are the chapters on transitioning from the full-time career track to living on a reduced income and workload. It's not all about the money. It requires thinking about how to find a new locus of identity, how to adjust to a spouse who stops working and lolls about enjoying coffee and reading the paper online while you're still commuting. What if both of you push your-selves out of the settled groove that has become so comfortable that you can just go through the motions? Yes, it's *un*comfortable to change chairs. But it can make you feel young again. It can even make you fall in love all over again. I know.

It happened for my husband and me when we uprooted our lives in our 60s and moved across the country to start again. Sure, we started off in a three-room faculty apartment fighting over the single bathroom. But we also found an outdoor running track that overlooked San Francisco Bay and an ocean with seemingly infinite horizons. That's when I began writing my book *Passages in Caregiving*. Before we changed our lives, my husband had been diagnosed with non-Hodgkin's lymphoma. Five years after we changed, the lymphoma was gone, and it never returned. My hus-band had a bonus life of 15 years as a teacher-guru.

Spontaneity, the hallmark of childhood, is well worth cultivat-ing to counteract the rigidity that may otherwise set in as we grow older. I'm thinking about a male friend of mine who in his early 60s had two divorces behind him and was settled into retirement and bachelorhood. But the woman he was seeing and loving insisted that she wanted to get married and have a child. Spontaneously, he said, "Sure, why not?" Today, as a widower in his early 80s, the light of his life is his 22-year-old son. The widower's roadmap had to be redrawn, so he went back to work as a freelance editor. That, he says, will pay for the pleasure of seeing his son through law school.

Yes, there will always be surprises for which we cannot plan, both good and not so good. But if you have marked up this work-book with a roadmap that makes sense for you, the chances are good that you won't bury your head in the sand or run into a sand trap and get stuck. I wish you an exciting journey.

Gail Sheehy
March 2013

Introduction

At an AARP forum I attended not too long ago, author Gail Sheehy spoke about her husband's battle with a debilitating illness. At one point, she related, the palliative care doctor came to their house and asked her husband, "What are your goals for this stage in life?"

I don't recall the response, but it was the question itself, posed to someone who clearly had life-threatening problems, that struck me.

I was in my 60s at the time and thought, "What are *my* goals at this stage in my life? Do I even have any goals?"

The doctor's question led me to think about the rest of my life. If all goes well, I thought, I still have another third of it to live. I realized that it might be a good thing to consider my vision for the next 25, 30, or more years—and then it occurred to me that I had none.

Gail's husband had an answer. I hadn't even considered the question.

■ ■ ■

When we were kids, I always had a goal. When asked, "What are you going to be when you grow up?" my answer was easy: "Shortstop for the New York Yankees." That answer changed over time as I considered other interesting careers: cowboy, firefighter, doctor, lawyer, teacher, and so on. I always had an answer, and reality didn't matter much.

The question persisted as I grew older and soon was accompanied by "What will you major in?" My answer to that also changed many times, even after I was *in* college and had chosen a major. Each time I came up with an answer, I was totally sure it was the right one, even if that certainty lasted only days. Frankly, it was pretty easy to come up with an answer. I looked around, saw what looked cool, and tried it on. I liked the visions in my head of roping a steer, of dragging the big hose to the flaming building, and of receiving the Nobel Prize for discovering the cure for cancer—but for a long time hitting the home run in the bottom of the ninth in the seventh game of the World Series stayed at the top of the list.

In short, I had a goal.

I had always had a goal. I also had role models, perhaps, four or five. My father, mother, brother, friend, teacher, boss—all people I emulated at one time or another.

Throughout my adulthood and professional life, I continued to have goals: the better job, the next book, the senior league softball championship. And I continued to have role models: the great boss, the creative genius, and the older shortstop.

Fast-forward to middle age, the time we're supposed to start planning for our lives as senior citizens. Now my contemporaries and I jokingly ask ourselves, "What do we want to be when we grow up?" I'm already grown up, and although I've finally eliminated shortstop for the Yankees, I'm not as sure as I was about my answer. I could have another 25, 30, or more years to live (my father died at 96!). I hope that most of them will be as a relatively healthy, active guy. But the question of what to be when I grow up is a whole lot more meaningful when I think of myself facing decades without a full-time job or career path. The scary part of all of this is that, for the first time in my life, I don't have any answers, I don't have any goals, and, frighteningly, I don't know who my role models are.

■ ■ ■

This book is not about retirement—for one thing, most of us aren't retiring, in the traditional sense—but about the question, "What are our goals for this stage in our lives?" I think we all know some of the answer: We want to be as healthy, happy, and wealthy as possible for as long as possible. We want to make sure we've done all we can to provide for our kids and loved ones, and we want to grab whatever joys there are to be had.

Introduction

But how do we do all those things? What can we do to maximize the chances that when the end is near, we can look back and feel good about it all?

The answer, at least in part, is by planning. This book will help you plan for your later years by focusing on your goals and your expectations. At the same time, it will provide the template you need to take care of legal, insurance, and other necessities that could easily become major barriers to achieving your goals.

I've looked hard at what my age means and realize it's not just about the actual number or my health. It's both of those, plus a lot more. Sure, I can't expect to dive for the ball while playing shortstop. But that doesn't mean I can't still participate. Or does it? And does that matter? Can I find another outlet to meet that long-established goal and joyful experience of competing on the ball field?

To establish my goals now, I first place myself in the appropriate spot on what I call a "level of activity" scale. We all know folks who play ball, ski, or run marathons well into their 80s. They are lucky to be able to pursue activities they obviously love. We know people who work in their chosen fields into their 90s because they love it and they can. But what about those who have health, financial, or other limitations? What about those who just prefer a less active lifestyle?

I gave up playing softball when I couldn't see the ball as well as I used to and became the guy they put out in right field. So what? Instead of feeling depressed about it and becoming inactive, I moved my attention to other things, as so many of us do. I discovered a new team sport. It requires some physical ability, but within my health limitations: I'm a dog handler in the sport of dog agility.

I now train my young border collie to run through tunnels, over jumps, and around weave poles. I'm not a very good handler yet—I'm in the little league of the sport. But again, so what? This sport gives me the chance to establish a new goal for myself at this stage in life. As I realize that becoming a good agility handler means a new focus for me, I think about Gail Sheehy's husband and his goals for the time he had left. It's from this perspective that I think of getting older as a good thing, presenting me with new opportunities and new challenges ahead.

■ ■ ■

I envision the next 25 or 30 years through many filters. First, my marriage. My wife and I are diligent about communicating our individual visions. Fortunately, we continue to share similar ideas about our later years, and for the most part have the same likes, dislikes, and lifestyle goals.

The next filter is my family. I'm happy that my relatives live close by and are thus both near and dear. I love watching my grandchildren grow up—and even more importantly, being a part of their growing up.

Then there are the filters of finances and health. My wife and I are lucky to be relatively secure financially; we both planned long ago, and had sufficient income, to stash away some savings. We're both pretty healthy. Even though we've experienced some health issues that have limited our choices and put us in different places on the level of activity scale, neither of us is so limited that we can't find outlets we enjoy. We've thought long and hard about our leisure time and about our living arrangements.

We don't fear uncertainties about the future. We expect some, and through planning try to minimize the impact of big changes that are thrust upon us, aware that many of us are just an illness or accident away from losing the security we too often take for granted. We've organized our lives so that if a crisis hits, our financial obligations and commitments won't be too difficult for our survivors to figure out. We've written letters to our heirs explaining ourselves—our ideals and our wishes—that include information needed when we're gone. We hope our children don't have to read those letters too soon. But having written the letters comforts us.

The next filter is how we spend our time. Both my wife and I have transitioned successfully from full-time jobs and upwardly mobile career paths to part-time positions, allowing us more free time but not throwing us cold turkey into having no work, no anchor, or no helm to help us steer. Most people I have interviewed, however, express one particular concern about their later years: What will they to do with themselves to keep busy? Some dread the idea of lying on their couches with nothing more important to do than watching reruns. Others proclaim they hope to die at their desks. I hope they don't. I hope they allow themselves to broaden their visions into new worlds, to take on new roles. So many people—in particular those who had successful careers—formed their identities around their jobs or professions. They were lawyers, doctors, businesspeople, plumbers, carpenters, or teachers—but when they retired they were . . . nothing. At best, they were unsure of *what* they were. Retirement doesn't prevent them from being *who* they are. But it can prevent them from labeling themselves as anything but *older*. This segues to a question none of us likes to ask—a question that I think we must all ask ourselves, and one that I now ask you:

Are you getting older?

Well, yeah, in a literal sense, of course you are. But I invite you to dump the value judgment surrounding it. Getting older is not bad. Getting older simply means you're no longer young. Getting older is a good thing (as the joke says, it's better than the alternative). So stop denying your age; stop thinking that "old" is a dirty word. It's an adjective that merely says you've lived many years. It has nothing to do with what you can or can't do. It doesn't put limits on *who* you are (except that you can't be the American Idol or enlist in the armed services). Being older has its virtues too: You get senior discounts at certain ages at certain places; you can start tapping into your Social Security benefits and you're eligible for Medicare; if you've built up a nest egg, you may be able to enjoy more leisure time.

In this book, you'll read about the things you have to do and the steps you have to take to establish goals and roles for this time of your life. With my step-by-step approach, worksheets, notes, tips, warnings, and personal stories, I'll get you through those administrative, legal, and financial challenges so you can focus on the key question, "What are your goals for this stage in life?" To get there, you'll find your place on the level of activity scale.

Then you can address all the other options you'll have, whether it's about where you choose to live, the relationships you have with family and friends, the kinds of activities you get involved in, and your work and work hours. All of these issues will affect and be affected by your financial strength and health.

■ ■ ■

So follow along as I present this roadmap for living the rest of your life. On this journey I provide you with smart choices about your money, health, work, and lifestyle. And I will give you tools to help you pursue your dreams. As the map unfolds, you will learn about a level of activity scale and about staying fit and healthy. The map will take you through health insurance options, including Medicare and long-term care insurance. We'll visit the transition from career track to part-time work or retirement and present creative ways to maintain an active leisure time. We'll look at financial planning to help you make your money last. And we'll discuss estate planning—that is, providing for your heirs—including what to include in the talk with your heirs so they know all they need to know about your legal and business affairs. From there, the roadmap will take you through a discussion of the various home- and living-arrangement options you have. Our final destination will look at the relationships we have with family and friends, and how those relationships affect the decisions we make. At this last stop on our roadmap, I'll talk about complex family arrangements, blended families, caregiving for our loved ones, remarriages, prenuptial agreements, and how things might be different for those who are unmarried and those who do not have children. And I'll discuss the idea of providing a legacy through charitable giving and the use of an ethical will or a letter to our survivors and loved ones.

Throughout the journey, you'll learn from people I interviewed whose words and actions provide guidance and who, perhaps, will serve as a role model for you. And you'll read about ideas you can try on for size. As was told to me many years ago, *if it fits, it's yours.*

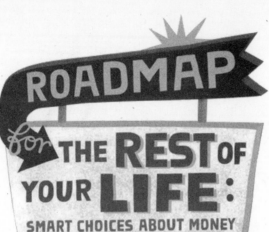

ROADMAP for THE REST OF YOUR LIFE: SMART CHOICES ABOUT MONEY HEALTH, WORK, LIFESTYLE... AND PURSUING YOUR DREAMS

CHAPTER

Where Are You on the Level of Activity Scale?

■ ■ ■

In this chapter, I introduce a different way to look at yourself by focusing on your lifestyle and your abilities.

While watching me work out at the gym the other day, an acquaintance said, "Not only don't you look your age but you're also not acting your age." I laughed and thanked him. I was reminded of when, years ago, Gloria Steinem announced on national TV that she was 40 (she's now in her 70s). The audience gasped. People couldn't believe that this beautiful, glamorous woman was over 40. Her remark to the audience was, "Folks, *this* is what 40 looks like!" But she could have also said, "Folks, *this* is what 40-year-olds *act* like!"

We have so many preconceived notions of age. And it starts early. When we were celebrating my birthday, I asked my grandson, who was about 7 at the time, how old he thought I was. He said, "50." I said, "No, quite a bit more." He replied, "100?" Yikes. Well, how would he know what to guess? Whether 50 or 100, the numbers didn't mean anything to him. They mean something to us only because we have so many preconceived notions of age.

We all know people who play ball, ski, run marathons, and work out religiously well into their 70s or 80s. Others continue to work well past traditional retirement age. They stay active and in good physical shape. "But they don't act 80," you might say. That's because they don't live by the same chronological rules that others do. Through good genes, some luck, a lot of hard work, and great motivation, they continue to do what they love.

At the same time, some people cannot engage in physical activity because of health problems, injuries, or other limitations. Yet, they may be equally motivated and have a very active, almost high-intensity lifestyle. Other people may not enjoy physical exercise or exertion but live anything but a sedate life. They may travel extensively, work long hours, and volunteer a great deal of their free time. Their lifestyle is very active but not necessarily physically exerting.

Life Story

My friend Mitch, who had polio as a child and again in his 50s, walked with crutches for several years before needing a wheelchair to get around. At first reluctant to use the wheelchair, Mitch soon found it to be indispensable. It changed his life, he told me. For the first time in years, he was able to do things that he hadn't been able to do for so long. From the moment he decided to use that chair, a new world opened to him. He could now go to the store without pain. He could attend baseball games, concerts, movies, and parties. And he could take his dog to the dog park, which is where I met him. In his 50s, he went from being practically housebound to active. Despite the wheelchair, his level of activity actually increased.

So when we think about how we plan to live the rest of our lives, one of the key factors to consider is the degree to which we want to and can be active.

Adapting this concept to our often age-obsessed society leads us to a different measure of who we are, which I call the level of activity (LOA) scale. How do we define this? There are no hard rules for this measure but rather a range. It's not chronological—that is, we don't go from one LOA to another simply by having lived another year. In fact, if we are so motivated, we can move up the ladder to a higher LOA as we age chronologically. The 55-year-old woman who decides to train for a 100-mile bike ride but who hasn't done this kind of physical exertion in years would increase her LOA. And the previously active 50-year-old who suffers a debilitating injury or severe back pain may change how he spends his leisure time, lowering his LOA level to one in which he coaches instead of plays.

The point is that when we define ourselves—and when others define us—we very often start with our age. That puts us in a cubbyhole that can be hard to break out of.

As you think about living the rest of your life, it's often good to start with defining your lifestyle.

Defining Your Lifestyle

Table 1.1 lists the level of activity number in the first column and sample activities or approaches to life corresponding to each LOA number. A marathoner who is constantly on the go, for example, would have an LOA number of 1, while someone who has difficulty getting around or requires assistance to do so, and who does not lead an active lifestyle, would be at level 8. An athlete who competes in sports while in a wheelchair could very well be at level 1 or 2. The point is that it's not your chronological age or your skill level that defines who you are. Rather, your ability and desire to participate within a range of activity, whether relaxed or intense, better defines your limits, which, in turn influences your choices.

In addition, and perhaps more importantly, it's neither your chronological age nor your level of activity score that totally defines you. But both of those are factors that may influence what you choose to do—just as the wheelchair-bound athlete will ski or play basketball, so too the 50-year-old man who can participate in a sport, and is in good enough shape to do so, may want to spend a great deal of his leisure time reading or being involved in some other quiet activity such as stamp collecting. Some folks may work a full day and head home to plop in front of the TV. Some retired people may be involved in various civic and volunteer activities and are busier and more active than they've ever been. The lifestyle you prefer influences your choices just as much as your level of activity.

Table 1.1 Level of Activity (LOA) Scale

Level of Activity Score	Activity Level	Explanations and Examples of Activity Level
1	Extremely high	Always on the go; a Type-A personality. Extremely high energy. Can exercise or play sports regularly. Can run a marathon; do any of the legs of a triathlon; sprint 100 yards; play consecutive rounds of golf; ski five days in a row; play two or three sets of singles tennis two or three times a week; work six or seven days a week for 10 to 12 hours a day.
2	Very high	Very high energy and stamina. Can engage in full cardio workout three times a week; play multiple sets of tennis or two rounds of golf, walking the course, a day; jog or power walk routinely; participate in athletic events; work long hours including weekends.
3	High	High energy and stamina. Can play doubles tennis or a round of golf, walking the course, two or three times a week; work out, with an hour of cardio, two or three times a week; jog regularly for 20 to 30 minutes; bicycle 50 miles every month or so; work normal hours plus some weekends.
4	Moderate	Good energy and stamina; more of a Type-B personality. Can exercise once or twice a week, including some cardio; play golf or doubles tennis once or twice a week; work normal hours plus occasional late nights or weekends.
5	Less than moderate	Some energy and stamina. Can play a round of golf using a cart; climb several flights of stairs without losing breath; ride a stationary bike or do cardio exercise periodically for a half hour; work normal hours.
6	Minimal	Minimal energy and stamina; lives a relatively sedate life. Can run short distances with effort or climb one flight of stairs without losing breath; work full or part time.
7	Somewhat limited	Limited energy and stamina. Can walk with no assistance but limited in distance and slope; maneuver easily and walk up a limited number of stairs; work part time or not at all.
8	Very limited	Can move around with crutches, a walker, or a wheelchair; work part time or not at all.

Note

In determining your level of activity, avoid making value judgments. Someone who reads a great deal and prefers a sedate lifestyle is not "bad;" nor is the para-athlete "good." People make choices about how to live their lives because of individual likes, dislikes, and abilities. You don't have to fall into the trap of labeling a lifestyle bad or good.

The LOA explanations are, of course, merely examples of the degrees of exertion as well as the degrees of intensity you have chosen to live your life. Type-A people who have worked long hours every day for years but aren't athletic might still put their LOA at level 1. If you, like millions of aging baby boomers, work all day in construction or other manual labor, or if you regularly bicycle but wouldn't consider running (and many people who have bad knees, hips, or backs are warned not to jog), you can place yourself in one of the top rows. The LOA scale provides one view of who you are, and that view can help you focus on your future.

Creating LOA-Specific Goals

Why define your chosen lifestyle with a level of activity scale? For one simple reason: The person you are now, and generally the person you have been for most of your adult life, likely predicts the person you will be for the rest of your life. Although there are many exceptions, it follows that if you've been a high-intensity worker, athlete, or participant in leisure activities, there's a pretty good chance your approach to life takes high-intensity focus. As a result, unless you decide to, or have to, make a radical change, you're probably not going to last too long living a quiet, sedate, hangin'-out-on-the-beach lifestyle. Or if you do choose to live on the beach, you'll likely spend your time surfing, boating, and windsurfing. You'll probably want the option to do lots of things nearby, perhaps a vibrant nightlife or lots of cultural opportunities (especially if you have injuries or conditions that limit your physical activity).

At the same time, there is no hard and fast rule that you can't adapt or change your lifestyle. If you are one of the lucky ones with enough resources, you can try a different lifestyle doing something you think might be a good fit, or something you've long dreamed of. If it doesn't work, well, at least you tried. There are many examples of people trying one thing and discovering later that they prefer something different. Just look at the story of John and Andrea in the Life Story sidebar.

Life Story

Ten years ago, John and Andrea, now in their 50s, sold their successful business in New England and moved to a small beach community in North Carolina. They rented for a year while their new home was built, during which they spent most of their time overseeing the construction, getting to know the community and the other residents, and involving themselves in local activities. John became active with the country club and Andrea became a volunteer firefighter. After the house was completed, they both felt they needed more to do, so John got his real estate license and joined a brokerage. Andrea began painting. Fast-forward five or six years, when they felt what they were doing still wasn't satisfying enough, so they opened a restaurant.

Both had been high-intensity small business owners, always on the go, participating in their community, leading an active lifestyle. They never felt comfortable with the notion of leisure time. They are both extremely happy with the new venture and with the busy, active lifestyle to which they've returned.

The point of John and Andrea's story deserves some emphasis: Unless you have the resources to make multiple life changes, think carefully about choosing a lifestyle that's radically different from the one you're used to. This is true for how you spend your leisure time, how close you live to your family—or how easy it is for them to continue to be part of your life—and the costs associated with the new lifestyle. In later chapters, I explore these issues and choices you can make regarding each scenario. And of course, consider your LOA score. While becoming less active is fairly common—whether through illness, injury, loss of muscle tone, or loss of drive—moving up the scale is also commonplace. As we've seen, many people get re-energized through rehabilitative services such as physical therapy. Others simply commit to a lifestyle in which old goals are readjusted or new goals formed.

Life Story

As I approached my fiftieth birthday, people warned me that I would soon have a midlife crisis. I often joke that instead of buying a sports car or seeking a mistress, I rode my bike 330 miles in four days for an AIDS ride.

I had never done anything quite so athletic, but I had been attending spinning classes in my gym and felt I was ready to commit to the challenge. Raising the required funds was a snap—almost all my friends quickly pledged financial support—but the training was especially difficult since I was overweight and not in the best of shape. I joined a team to help me, and my wife and friends were also supportive. I trained for months and, as the four-day ride approached, I was beginning to feel confident. My training partners encouraged me, and one even agreed to be my tent-mate. The ride was difficult, and I was never certain of making it all the way. But make it I did, and at the closing ceremony I triumphantly hoisted my bike over my head in celebration, just as my fellow riders were doing. I haven't done anything like that AIDS ride again, but by committing myself to and completing the training program, I upped my LOA score.

Similarly, you might choose to change your level of activity because your relationship status changes. Suppose, for example, a relationship you've been in for a long time ends, and you're now single. In time, you might find that the lifestyle you led for many years was more attuned to your partner's wishes rather than your own. For the sake of the relationship, you lived in a particular area, participated in certain activities, or spent a great deal of your leisure time with your partner's family. If that changes, you could imagine a totally different set of goals and expectations, one that takes you traveling more (or less), doing new things with your time, or changing your professional life.

As your financial situation changes, it's important to reassess your LOA. Imagine that your partner dies, leaving you with a significant sum of money. Or, in the alternative, the partner who once provided the sole income for your household dies, and now you have to live on your own resources. You're very likely to change the way you spend your leisure time, where you choose to live, the people you get together with, and perhaps your professional life, if you no longer have to work or now *must* or want to work. The addition or subtraction of financial resources could significantly alter your lifestyle, either giving you the freedom to do more or less, or limiting what you can do.

Conclusion

One of the most important decisions you can make involves choosing a level of activity and a lifestyle that best suits you. Where you place yourself on the level of activity scale has an impact on other life choices you make and can be as important as your finances, health, relationships, and goals.

In Chapter 2, "What Are Your Goals for This Stage in Life?" I discuss how your level of activity score affects your goals. I provide guidance for creating goals (or realizing what they already are). And I focus on ways to find appropriate, inspiring role models.

CHAPTER

What Are Your Goals for This Stage in Life?

■ ■ ■

Once you determine your level of activity, you are in a better position to plan for the rest of your life: to decide where to live, how to manage your career, how long and how much to work, what activities to pursue in your leisure time, how you can best achieve your financial goals, how to approach health care and fitness, and how to ensure your estate—that is, everything you own—is passed to the next generation.

In the introduction to this book, I mentioned how I was struck by the fascinating and provocative question the palliative care doctor asked Gail Sheehy's husband, who was suffering from a debilitating medical condition: "What are your goals for this stage in life?"

In this chapter, I focus on that question and one related to it. Both will help in the decision-making process to address your long-term plans. These two questions go hand and hand and are not necessarily sequential:

1. What are my goals for this stage in life?
2. Who are my role models?

Creating Your Life Goals

In the introduction, I also talked about how, when we were kids, adults were always asking, "What do you want to be when you grow up?" Our answers usually changed as we grew a little older. For me, cowboy or firefighter became doctor or lawyer (although shortstop always made the list). We had little idea what it meant to actually *be* a doctor or lawyer and certainly less idea of what it took to get there. Nevertheless, we had an answer.

Later in life, if we pursued college, the question changed to "What do you want to major in?" It's the same question, really, and both boil down to a more general question: "What is your goal?" We were forced to make decisions. You couldn't just go to college; you had to choose which college—and part of that choice was based on what program you wanted to enroll in. You couldn't just sign up for random classes; you had to matriculate toward a degree. That meant taking a core curriculum and earning enough credits in your major so you could graduate in a reasonable amount of time. Sometimes with the help of an adviser, sometimes on our own, we moved our way through school with an objective in mind: graduate, then either go on to more schooling or go out into the world and work. In our serious moments, we reflected on what that might be like to leave the confines of school. Maybe we were terrified, maybe we were excited. Most likely it was a combination of the two. We took solace in knowing we weren't the only ones facing adulthood and all the uncertainties that would bring.

Once we entered the workforce and, for some of us, married and began to raise a family, we took life step by step. Sometimes we moved sideways, sometimes backward. Always we hoped we were moving forward. Through internships, observation, and jobs, some of us got an inkling—or more—of what it was like to actually work as a doctor, a lawyer, a business professional, or even a shortstop. Some learned what it meant to be a parent.

Most of our goals were fairly clear and likely similar to what many others of our generation wanted: a job, a good job, a better job. You, like many of us, probably hoped you could be financially comfortable—or at least have a reliable income. You probably wanted to meet a life partner and have a family—to get through your kids' teenage years without going insane, put them through college without going broke, and hope they didn't move back in with you. Maybe you looked forward to having grandchildren, nieces, and nephews, and spoiling them rotten. In short, you had goals.

As you start to think about your later years, you might have a sense of what your new goals might be. If you've stopped working or reduced your hours, you may wake up in the morning and not know what to do with yourself all day. If you're still working, you may be thinking about whether you want to make some changes to make your life more fulfilling. If your level of activity has changed, you'll also want to reassess your goals.

Life Story

Jill had several careers in her life. Right after college, she worked in college administration. After a few years, she got married and started a family. While her three children were young, she focused her time and energy on being a mother and homemaker and then started a few small businesses, working part time at home. When the kids grew older, she moved back into the workforce and for 30-plus years held a series of more responsible jobs. Even when working in full-time, demanding jobs, she was involved in civic activities and had many good friends. The day arrived when her employer offered her the chance to retire with a golden handshake: six months' salary plus all the vacation days she had never used. Although she wasn't old enough to receive Social Security, she calculated that the severance pay plus the unemployment insurance she would receive as a result of being laid off would carry her up to the age she could qualify for Social Security. Jill jumped at this chance.

Her daily routine changed, of course, but was remarkably full. She became a gym rat, going almost every day for an hour or two. She frequently visited with her friends, cooked meals for her family, and planned future travels to exotic places. She was busy most of the time.

After several months, she sat down and realized that on most days she had about four or five hours where she had nothing to do. It gnawed at her and she confessed, "I don't know what to do with those free hours every day." When asked, "What are your goals?" she responded, "I don't really have any. Maybe it would be good to start thinking about that."

Roadmap for the Rest of Your Life

In my interviews for this book, I found that people who were no longer working full time were most concerned about what to do with leisure time. I discuss leisure time options in greater depth in Chapter 7, but it's important here to pinpoint this concern and tie it to the question, "What are your goals for this stage in life?"

An Internet search for setting or creating life goals yields hundreds of thousands of hits. Many search results provide excellent suggestions and reveal similarities. Following are my own 10 steps geared to help you answer the question, "What are your goals in life?" These steps combine the best advice offered by numerous sources along with those that have worked best for me. If they work for you, that's great. If not, or if you find others that I didn't include, I encourage you to contact me through my website, www.bartastor.com, so we can make the list better for everyone.

Ten Steps to Creating Your Life Goals

1. **Observe yourself.**

   What you are doing is, for the most part, what you want to be doing. It's who you are and what you have chosen. This isn't some existential philosophy; it's simply an observation. So the first step in creating your life goals is to see what activities and interests you've already chosen, what has generally turned you on, and what you notice you can do for a period of time during which you are focused and involved and not counting the minutes until it's over.

2. **Brainstorm.**

   Using what you've noted already about your current behavior, think of everything that interests you. Let your mind wander, and try not to filter out things that you think may be silly or unrealistic. If you're stuck, say the first thing that pops into your head. Creative teams often use brainstorming to create goals, emphasizing that there is no bad idea, nothing stupid, and nothing absurd. Judgments about the quality and usefulness of an idea can come later.

3. **Visualize.**

   Take what you've discovered in the first two steps and imagine yourself engaged in the activity or having achieved a goal. What does it look like? Close your eyes and daydream;

12

let your mind create the scenario. If running a marathon pops up, for example, envision yourself running mile after mile after mile, alone. Is it still interesting to you? If so, great. If not, and if you're thinking about having *completed* the marathon—that is, at the finish line or the next week telling folks about having accomplished it—well, that says something different, doesn't it? Nothing wrong with that— it's not "bad" to feel that pride. It's just that the accomplishment, not the activity itself, is what's important for you. I mentioned in Chapter 1 that several years ago, I rode a 330-mile bike ride in four days. My goal was to accomplish the ride and support the fight against AIDS. Frankly, I didn't like much of the actual ride. But I loved having succeeded.

4. **Don't judge yourself.**

Throughout this process, avoid labeling your ideas or thoughts as good, bad, or anything else, and don't apply such value judgments to yourself. If you're struggling to create a list, don't conclude that you can't. Don't make more of this than what it is: a list of potential goals. If nothing comes right away, relax. That's fine. Those goals will come as you complete some of the other steps. Judging yourself will suppress your creativity. At this stage you're exploring possibilities, not honing a final product.

5. **Observe others.**

There's not much new in the world, at least in the large sense. So whatever your goal might be, somebody else has had it. If you find someone else doing something that intrigues you, or pursuing a goal that strikes a chord with you, try it on. If it fits, it's yours. Goals aren't proprietary.

6. **Be specific.**

You don't need to think big, but you do need to think specific. There's no difference between a small goal and a large one. And for this purpose, there's no difference between an accomplishment and a goal. At the same time, be as specific as you can, and also include a timeframe. If your goal or accomplishment is to create a part-time business for yourself, think about the number of hours you want to devote, the time it will take to learn the business, and what you will actually be *doing* during those hours. If you realize then that your goal was to *create* a business, not necessarily *run* a business, that knowledge itself is an accomplishment.

7. **Write it down.**

    When you create your list of goals, commit your thoughts and ideas to paper, either handwritten or on your computer—and include ways to measure whether you have achieved each goal. This is especially helpful when getting to the specifics. Don't limit yourself to a certain number of goals, even if your list is growing huge. When you read it all back, you might see patterns or similarities that will allow you to shorten the list. Or you might read something later and say to yourself, "What was I thinking? I don't even like doing that."

8. **Include others.**

    Sharing your ideas with other people can be tricky but worthwhile. By confiding in others, you take a risk, and yet running your unfiltered thoughts and dreams by a partner, close friend, or colleague, especially at this point, can provide useful feedback. You might, for instance, say something like this: "In the back of my mind, I've always had this notion of learning to fly. It's bizarre because I usually don't even like traveling and never liked commercial flying. But flying a small plane just seems different. Does that sound ridiculous?" Be open to any feedback.

9. **Analyze conflicting goals.**

    It's possible that one of your ideas and potential goals will conflict with another. For example, "I want to get myself more financially stable within two or three years and set up a savings program" might be one of your objectives. A potential conflict might be, "I want to remodel my kitchen within the next year." You may find ways to accomplish both, or perhaps they really are at odds. So you can either try to figure out a way to achieve both simultaneously or decide to put one off for later. You may realize that setting up a savings program has to take priority over remodeling the kitchen.

10. **Categorize your thoughts.**

    Consider different aspects of your life when thinking about your goals: family, career, level of activity, finances, health, social and cultural opportunities, education, retirement, and so forth. Some of your goals, ideas, and thoughts will overlap in two or more areas; some will just apply to one area. Categorizing your goals will help you think and plan more creatively; it will help you get "unstuck" and encourage you to be specific.

After completing these 10 steps, you should be ready to draft a list of the goals you are ready to pursue. For now, focus on creating your framework. Remember that setting goals is different from achieving goals. My focus in this book is to help you set goals. Once you do that, a myriad of books and articles can help you find ways to achieve them.

Now that you have your basic list, you can fill in the details for each goal by answering these questions:

- What do I know or have to learn?
- Where can I get the information?
- What skills do I need to master?
- What other resources are available?
- What are my benchmarks?
- Who can help me achieve my goal?

The next section focuses on that last question.

Finding Role Models

Traditionally, the role models we emulate are usually older than we are, and most often of the same gender. As we mature, we may find role models who are younger or of the opposite sex. Over the years, at one time or another, my father, my brother, a friend, a teacher, a boss, a sport's hero, and a celebrity have served as my role models. The role models I chose had certain qualities and characteristics I admired. That's not to say I wanted to be just like them, but I wanted to possess the specific traits, strengths, attitudes, and behaviors that I held in high regard.

I had bosses and colleagues whom I thought had it all together, and I looked up to them and copied them when appropriate. For example, when Chuck, one of the best bosses I ever had, placed his trust in me, I wanted to do the same and treat people I supervised with equal respect. Chuck hired me for a director-level job and after a few weeks went on vacation, leaving me to fend for myself. I expressed my panic and his response was, "Don't worry, you'll be fine. And when I come back I'll help you pick up the pieces." He knew I'd make some mistakes. But he also knew everything was repairable. He had a great perspective I so admired. He'd reassure me, "There are only three kinds of emergencies: for one you call the police; for another you call the fire department; and for the third you call the ambulance. Everything else is not an emergency."

That kind of management style, and the wisdom behind it, rang true to me, and I wanted to take it on. It fit, so it became mine.

As I grew older and talked with scores of my peers, I learned that many of us share a concern that we no longer have role models for this next stage of our life. Who do you see in front of you that's living the life you might envision for yourself? Is there anyone?

Do you, like many of us, feel as if you are breaking new ground, looking ahead to the next stage of life without a role model to emulate?

Life Story

Jill, who realized as a newly retired person that she needed to establish more goals if she was to fill her idle hours, said she didn't have any role models. When younger, she said, her mother, older sister, teachers, and friends served as role models. But somewhere along the line, that stopped. Her mother had passed away—although many years earlier had ceased to be a role model. Jill had many of the same friends she had as a younger woman, but now she no longer thought of them as role models. Certainly she no longer worshipped movie stars or other celebrities. But she couldn't see any other role models in her life. When asked about it, she shrugged and said, "I live my life on much more of a day-to-day basis now, and the idea of having anyone I look up to, well, it's just not something I think about." When pressed, however, she admitted that indeed, she admired several people who possessed the qualities she emulated. Were they, then, role models? I asked. "Yes, I guess they are," Jill replied. She just never thought of these people as role models, just as people she admired.

Do we really need role models to guide the way when we're forging new pathways, trying something new, or uncertain of what lies ahead? I think the answer is yes.

It's also important to realize that our relationships with role models involve some reciprocity: Leaders and mentors benefit from the reinforcement of their followers, and in that sense stay inspired to foster a new generation of role models.

So how do we go about finding role models? Here are five tips to help you find yours.

Five Tips for Finding Role Models

1. **Focus on individual traits and behaviors, not the whole person.**

   At this point in your life, there's probably no one person you want to be just like. But there are individual aspects of a person you admire or who is in a position that you want for yourself.

2. **Observe yourself.**

   Looking at yourself and your behavior is as important in finding role models as it is when creating your goals. Note the aspects of yourself you are most proud of as well as those that are not your best attributes. If you find that you tend to overreact when someone cuts you off on the expressway, for example, you can note that. Then, let's say, you see someone who manages to deal with anger in a more relaxed way, whether on the highway or in the workplace, a way that allows that person's anger to well up but be expressed diplomatically. If you think that person's method for managing outrage might work for you, consider that person a potential role model. Similarly, if you once handled yourself well in a type of situation that doesn't often present itself—let's say you were terrific in a high-pressure negotiation but you haven't been part of one recently—then find others who have that skill. By looking at them as role models, you can reinforce aspects of yourself that you like.

17

3. **Look for a good communicator.**

    It's one thing to admire someone or someone's attributes or behavior, but an ideal role model is someone you can form a relationship with, not just someone you gaze at through a window of respect. The more you can communicate with your role models and learn what makes them tick, the better and more significant they will be in continuing to shape your own behavior.

4. **Look for someone who is confident.**

    Good role models are people who are secure and confident in their opinions and beliefs, and proud of their ability to set and achieve their own goals. I can't remember ever having a role model who was wishy-washy or blasé about anything. Good role models are confident leaders who generally forge ahead but remain sensitive and concerned about the consequences.

5. **Look for someone who is open and willing to be a role model.**

    People you choose to serve as a role model should want to *be* one. Their confidence will be easier to recognize and emulate if they are willing to share their positive attitudes and attributes, and the guidance they provide will be more meaningful.

Conclusion

In this chapter, I asked the question, "What are your goals for this stage in life?" I explained how that question, posed to Gail Sheehy's husband, who was in need of palliative care, started me to think about my own goals. Realizing that I didn't have—or at least hadn't articulated—any goals, I started my roadmap by asking many friends and colleagues about their goals. I was curious, not just about what their goals were but how they came to be. Out of those discussions came the 10 steps to creating your life goals.

An important part of creating goals involves recognizing the possibilities. After all, how can you choose wisely—or even at all—without understanding what is *possible?* Often our goals reflect what we see in others, in particular, our role models. When I ask my peers about their role models, most say they don't really have them, at least not anymore. I say they have role models but have yet to focus on identifying them; similarly, and not surprisingly to me, people I've talked with have been hazy about envisioning their goals. So I provide tips for finding role models, because I think they can help us formulate goals.

In the next chapter, "Staying Healthy for the Rest of Your Life," I take a turn on the roadmap and focus on well-being. I cover a wide range of topics that form a foundation of living the rest of your life.

Staying Healthy for the Rest of Your Life

■ ■ ■

Age may be relative, but getting older is not. Everyone is different, and the aging process affects people differently, but certain characteristics of aging are common to most people. Among our goals, of course, are to live a healthy life as long as we can and to minimize the suffering we experience in our later years. It's critical that we do what we can to stay as healthy as we can. As my father used to say whenever he had a new audience—borrowing a quote attributed to both Mickey Mantle and Eubie Blake (who ironically, lived to be 100)—"If I knew I was going to live this long, I would have taken better care of myself."

In this chapter, I talk about ways to stay as healthy as possible in body, mind, and spirit. I cover these topics:

- Keeping fit by being active and eating well.
- Addressing common conditions such as "senior moments," dental disease, failing eyesight, and loss of hearing.
- Using medication and choosing a doctor.
- Dealing with depression, hot flashes, and increased sensitivity to cold.

This chapter describes what to expect and what to look for as you assess whether or not the physical or mental changes you experience requires treatment.

Keeping Fit and Young at Heart

Let me remind you of an important point I raised in the discussion about the level of activity scale in Chapter 1: Fit does not mean youthful. Today, adults of all ages run marathons, pump iron, and master stairs and step aerobics in health clubs. The point is that our goal is *not* to be young again. There's nothing wrong with getting older. Many people in their middle or senior years say they wouldn't trade their age for anything. They love being exactly who they are: a composite of all the experiences amassed over a lifetime.

You obviously can't stop time and you can't stop aging. But you may be able to delay some or all of the physical changes that comes with getting older.

One of the best ways to do that, for most people, is through exercise: a regular, appropriate routine. For example, many physicians and therapists feel strongly that a regular routine of exercise reduces the degree of osteoporosis. In particular, they recommend strengthening exercises using weights. Recent studies suggest that regular exercise is also helpful in preventing, lessening, or at least delaying, the effects of dementia, including Alzheimer's disease.

Note

Everyone starting an exercise program, regardless of their age, should be certain it is an appropriate routine for their age and physical condition. Consult a medical professional before starting any exercise regime.

Setting Goals for Exercise

What do I mean by a regular, appropriate exercise routine? Simply put, it includes three ingredients:

1. Aerobic activity for a healthy heart and lungs.
2. Flexibility exercises to keep muscles and joints moving smoothly.

3. Strengthening exercises to maintain muscle tone, halt bone loss, and prevent injury.

Consult with your medical advisers as you design your specific regimen. Find a routine you enjoy doing and look forward to, and choose activities you can do often and with little hassle; otherwise, it will be much too easy to put them off.

Let me emphasize that if you have limited mobility or require assistance, physical exercise can still be an essential part of your life, as any physical therapist will say, to maintain muscle strength and flexibility. Be sure you work closely with a specialist and together map out an exercise routine that fits into your lifestyle and that you can commit to.

Walking Walking is one of the best activities you can do regularly that incorporates the three essential ingredients: aerobic, flexibility, and strengthening. If your level of activity score suggests that walking is an acceptable activity, there are many ways to do it. You can simply walk around your neighborhood. Many communities offer trails designated for walkers and bike riders, so you don't have to walk on the sidewalk or in the street. Trails are great for getting exercise and socializing. (If there's a path or trailhead near your house, there's likely to be someone limbering up to walk briskly from one end to another.) If hot, cold, or bad weather derails you, you can use a treadmill at a gym or community center.

Another option is mall walking. More and more people, dressed in workout clothes and walking shoes, take to the shopping malls—often in the morning hours before the stores open—for a walk. This is especially true in inclement weather. Admittedly, most of them are retirees, but you don't have to be "old" to walk at the mall. I think it's important to stay away from value judgments and preconceived notions and not to be concerned about what others think about whether an exercise program (or any behavior, for that matter) is acceptable for you. Younger people can walk the mall for exercise, too. It all has to do with where you are on the LOA scale and your schedule.

The benefits of mall walking are enormous. You'll have things to look at and other people with whom you can interact. That in itself can make walking more enjoyable. Furthermore, mall walking costs nothing. No gym dues means significant savings for someone who may be concerned about making ends meet.

In some malls, an organized club or association might sponsor a walking program or, at least, keep it safe and supervised.

To learn more about mall walking, check with the central administration office of a nearby mall or your local senior community center.

Tip

If you're a gym rat, jogger, bicyclist, or sports fanatic, chances are you're aware of the problems and injuries you can sustain by insisting that "no pain is no gain." Strenuous exercise should never cause pain. If something hurts, stop what you're doing. Make sure you're not injured before resuming the activity— with caution. To be safe, check with your doctor or medical professional.

Working Out, Jogging, Bicycling, and More   Many of you may participate in various sports, either individually or on a team, or perform other strenuous forms of physical activity, such as jogging, bicycling, swimming and doing other aerobic or weight-bearing exercises. If you regularly engage in strenuous exercise, you are most likely aware of the benefits, risks, and the challenges involved. If, however, you have not set up any kind of routine, schedule, or training program, I suggest you check out the opportunities at a local health club or community center. You can take all kinds of exercise classes at these places where instructors are usually able to accommodate people of all abilities. Always let the instructor know if this is the first time you're taking the class and any limitations you might have.

Note

Many health clubs and gyms offer reduced rates for those who are 55+ or 65+. Some clubs offer lower-cost limited memberships to people who will use the facilities during off-peak hours (e.g., between 9 A.M. and 4 P.M.). Some employers offer health insurance programs that provide rebates or reduced rates at local health clubs. Check with your employer's human resources department to see if you have that benefit in your health insurance package.

If you decide to train for a specific event or accomplishment—a 10k run or a century bike ride, for example—then consider contacting the clubs in your community that sponsor such activities. The people involved can often help you set up an appropriate training program and find training partners. A quick web search or an athletic-shoe or bike shop can point you to local clubs.

Keep in mind that there are many fitness and aerobic classes specifically designed for people 50+ offered through local community recreations centers, adult schools, senior centers, YMCAs and YWCAs, and houses of worship. These are usually low-cost or free, run by professionals, and supervised.

For more information about fitness for the 50+ crowd, visit the AARP website at aarp.org.

Note

If you have a physical disability, your doctor may not prescribe an exercise regime but may instead refer you to physical therapy at a facility. In many cases, all or part of a club membership or activities fee may be covered by health insurance or be tax deductible. Check this out with a tax adviser.

We Are What We Eat

One of the biggest challenges we face as we grow older is maintaining good eating habits and getting well-balanced meals. With obesity such a major problem in our country, health professionals place a great deal of emphasis on eating habits and their direct link to serious conditions such as heart disease and diabetes. Medical research also suggests that malnutrition, particularly among those people who are 50 and older, is a growing concern.

Maintaining a balanced diet is no less important for middle-aged and older people than it is for younger ones. In some ways, as we get older we need to be even more careful that we get all the nutrients we need. Below I list 10 reasons why nutritional requirements get more complicated as we get older.

Ten Reasons Why Poor Nutritional Habits Increase as We Age

1. Appetite is based largely on our senses: taste, smell, and sight in particular. But the senses are not as keen as we age, and these sensory deficits and insufficient internal cues lead to a decrease in appetite.

2. As our bodies age, we need different kinds of foods in different proportions. Yet most of us are fairly rigid in our eating habits and likes and dislikes. What we've always eaten (and like) is what we always *want* to eat, regardless of whether it is good for us or whether we're getting the nutritional value we need.

3. More of us take various medications, many of which change our appetite and body chemistry. Some drugs may even cause nausea or other gastrointestinal complications that decrease appetite. Sometimes the combination of drugs leads to decreased appetite or shortages of certain vitamins or minerals.

4. We may suffer from diseases, such as adult-onset diabetes, that require special nutritional care. Yet we may not always be able to keep up with what our bodies need as our conditions change.

5. We may have various aches and pains of unknown origin and sometimes just don't feel well. As a result, we don't want to prepare meals or even go to the trouble of eating.

6. More and more of us live alone and just don't bother shopping and cooking for ourselves, eating less or relying on processed and fast food.

7. Some of us become unable to shop or cook for ourselves, but don't let others know and ask for help.

8. Some of us are in the early stages of dementia, including Alzheimer's disease, or senility, which can lead to poor eating habits.

9. Depression, loneliness, confusion, alcoholism, and substance abuse, which affect an increasing number of adults, can lead to decreased appetite and poor eating habits.

10. More of us live on fixed incomes or experience worsening economic conditions. As a result, we buy and eat less, trying to save money wherever we can. This is especially true in a tough economy.

One of the most important things you can do to maintain good nutrition is to make healthy food choices. Here are 15 superfoods that experts recommend as we age:

1. Apples
2. Asparagus
3. Blueberries
4. Broccoli
5. Butternut squash
6. Dark chocolate (at least 70 percent cacao)
7. Coffee, including unroasted green coffee
8. Fava (broad) beans
9. Greek yogurt
10. Kale
11. Oatmeal
12. Olive oil
13. Pears
14. Quinoa
15. Salmon

You can find more suggestions for good nutrition, including meal plans and delicious recipes, in the *AARP New American Diet* by Dr. John Whyte (John Wiley & Sons, 2012).

Warning

With the ever-growing concern about adult-onset diabetes, most dieticians and physicians recommend limiting sugar intake, especially for people with a family history of diabetes. In addition, many professionals recommend limiting the intake of simple carbohydrates, which can also help to prevent or lessen the effects of high blood sugar.

Addressing Common Conditions

Senior Moments

No doubt we all experience some memory loss as we age. In fact, memory loss is one of the most worrisome concerns people have.

Refrains such as "where are my keys?" or, upon entering a room, "why did I come in here?" may become all too familiar. Blame these "senior moments" on the hippocampus, the area in the brain where information is stored, which shrinks as we age. As a result, we process data more slowly.

So, while some memory loss is normal, if you're concerned that it's something more, you'll want to ask three questions. First, how do you quantify normal loss? Second, when do you know that your memory loss is getting more serious? And third, what, if anything can you do to either prevent or at least slow the progression of this problem? This section is designed to help answer those questions.

Age-Associated Memory Impairment Normal memory loss at midlife and older includes things such as intermittently blanking on someone's name, forgetting what you had for dinner last night, or not recalling your password to an oft-used website. These are typically not early signs of senility or Alzheimer's. These memory lapses are, as the medical community calls them, "minor neuro-cognitive disorders." It's just not something you should fret over (and, of course, the more anxiety you develop over it, the worse it gets).

That's not to say that you shouldn't take note, especially if memory loss occurs more and more often. If you experience this type of short-term memory lapse often, consider some of the other possible causes: prescription and over-the-counter drugs you are taking, alcohol use, stressful conditions, illness (especially an infection), and lack of sleep. If none of these appear to be the cause and your condition seems to grow worse, it's a good idea to speak with your doctor.

Confusion and Dementia Most people lump confusion and dementia (including Alzheimer's disease) into one category. But they are different conditions, even though they involve a disorder in thinking and rational processing and may have physical causes. In brief, not all confused people are demented, but all demented people are confused. Here are definitions to help distinguish the two:

Confusion: Confused people are aware of, and often distressed by, their state. Confusion is typically a temporary condition.

Dementia: People with dementia rarely have insight into their condition. Dementia is often progressive and irreversible. Alzheimer's disease is one kind of dementia.

Infections can sometimes cause confusion. In particular, systemic infections like those of the urinary tract often are associated with confusion. If you or a loved one starts showing sudden signs of confusion, contact a physician to rule out or treat infection as the cause. Systemic infections can be very serious and even fatal if not treated.

Coping with serious memory loss in a loved one suffering from dementia is difficult. Watching that person exhibit the behaviors accompanying the disease can cause tremendous sadness. You might feel totally isolated and helpless as your loved one slips further and further away, becoming unrecognizable as the person you once knew.

Here are a few points to keep in mind:

- Dementia is not a normal part of aging. Not all older people experience dementia.
- If you or a loved one exhibits an increasing amount of confusion, disorientation, or wildly out of character behaviors check with a physician.
- Although current medications cannot cure Alzheimer's or stop it from progressing, they may help lessen symptoms, such as memory loss and confusion, for a limited time.
- Poor nutrition and certain side effects or combinations of medicines can lead to increased confusion that can look like dementia.

Here are a few steps you can take to keep your brain as fit as possible.

1. Keep physically active. Studies show that higher exercise levels can reduce dementia risk by 30 to 40 percent compared with low activity levels, and physically active people tend to maintain better cognition and memory than inactive people. Most experts recommend 150 minutes a week of moderate activity.

2. Exercise your brain, too. Crosswords and Sudoku work, according to the latest research. But learn new things, too: a new musical instrument or a new song, a new language.
3. Keep your stress levels low. Easier said than done, I know. But chronic stress increases the cortisol in your brain, which leads to impaired memory. Meditation has been shown to help lower stress.
4. Try the Mediterranean diet. Studies show that a diet rich in fish, vegetables, fruit, nuts, and beans can cut the risk of Alzheimer's.
5. Live a purposeful life. One study showed that people with clear intentions and goals at the start of the study were less likely to develop Alzheimer's disease over the following seven years.

The more you understand about dementia and Alzheimer's, the easier it will be for you to handle the problems associated with it. To learn more about Alzheimer's and support groups for families, you can call the local chapter of the Alzheimer's Association (look online or in the white pages of the phone book). Or you can contact the national headquarters:

Alzheimer's Association
225 N. Michigan Avenue, Floor 17
Chicago, IL 60601
1-800-272-3900

Your Dental Health

Dental problems and gum disease can also become more troublesome as we age. Dental and gum problems can be either a symptom of poor nutrition or a cause of poor nutrition, leading to even more serious illnesses. Dental problems are *not* an inevitable part of growing older.

Seven Reasons Why Tooth Decay Increases as We Age

1. Gums tend to recede and expose more root surfaces, which are prone to decay.

2. Old fillings and crowns break off or crack.
3. We naturally produce less saliva as we age, which means acids in foods we eat are not neutralized, food is not washed away as well, and dental tissues get less of the calcium and phosphorus they need.
4. Medications such as painkillers and those used to control incontinence and hypertension (high blood pressure) reduce the production of saliva, which alters the chemical balance in your mouth.
5. The constant changes in the shape and size of dental tissue as we age means dentures and artificial teeth no longer fit as well.
6. Older people, particularly those suffering from arthritis or similar diseases, cannot grasp toothbrushes and dental floss as easily.
7. Visual impairment leads to poorer dental hygiene simply because we may not be able to see areas of concern in our mouths.

But there is plenty that you can do to maintain good dental hygiene.

Nine Steps You Can Take to Improve Gums and Teeth

1. Visit a dentist at least twice a year.
2. Visually check your mouth for obvious signs of dental or gum disease.
3. Eat well-balanced meals.
4. Brush your teeth at least twice a day.
5. At least every six months, get a new, soft-bristled toothbrush or change the brush end of an electric toothbrush.
6. If you have arthritis or some other disease that limits hand and arm motion, talk with your hygienist, dentist, or occupational therapist about ways to make brushing easier. You may try these solutions:

   - Enlarge the toothbrush handle with sponges or bicycle grips.
   - Elongate the handle with a piece of wood.
   - Use an elastic band to attach the toothbrush to the hand.
   - Use an electric toothbrush to make brushing easier.

7. If you wear dentures, check that they are not loose.
8. If you have dry mouth, sip water, suck on hard candies (stick to sugarless), and use something on your lips to keep them moist.
9. If you have persistent bad breath, check with a dentist or doctor to see if it's caused by medication or disease.

Because Medicare does not pay for visits to dentists, many older people stop getting dental care. But if you can afford them, many dental insurance programs are available to Americans age 50 and over. If you're not covered under an employer-sponsored dental plan, you can do a web search for a plan in your area. You can learn more by reading about dental health and dental plans at www.aarp.org.

Your Vision

By the time we reach our forties and fifties, a lot of us have grown accustomed to wearing reading glasses. We've pretty much accepted that as we age, our arms become too short for us to read the newspaper. Bifocal and trifocal glasses are common, not to mention bifocal contact lenses. Simply put, most of us become more farsighted as we age because the lenses in our eyes are less able to adjust.

The correct medical term for farsightedness is presbyopia, as distinguished from myopia, which means nearsightedness. Supermarkets, drug stores, and bookstores stock reading glasses in varying strengths. These reading glasses are essentially magnifying glasses, and many of us progress from the low-power 1.25 to the high-power 3.5 before we need prescription strength. For many of us, this is enough, although we certainly need to visit the eye doctor periodically to check our eyes and to make sure any failing vision is not complicated by some other problem.

For middle-aged and older adults, failing vision is considerably more complicated for several reasons:

- More than 50 percent of people age 80 and older will have cataracts or have had cataract surgery, according to the National Institutes of Health.

- We are susceptible to other various diseases, such as glaucoma and macular degeneration, which could cause failing vision.
- Our eyes are more sensitive to glare, and we may not be able to focus as quickly.

Poor vision affects your quality of life and can result in driving accidents and falls. To preserve and protect your eyesight, it's important to see an eye doctor at least every other year and more often if you have specific vision and optical concerns.

In addition, you can take a few precautionary steps to address poorer vision as you age:

- Increase the wattage of the light bulbs in your house (but be careful not to exceed the manufacturer's suggested wattage for fixtures). A 100-watt bulb should be sufficient for reading.
- Keep hallways and stairs well lit and install switches at both the top and bottom of stairs.
- Install nightlights (especially the kind that light up even if the electricity goes out) in the bedroom and bathroom.
- Make sure there is adequate light over the kitchen counter and stove.
- Buy a large-button telephone.
- Enlarge the keyboard on smart phones.
- Read large-print books and newspapers.
- Enlarge the font on your computer, tablets, and e-readers.
- Take advantage of the many products on the market for people with poor vision. You can visit one of the retail outlets or browse through one of a host of catalogs that now offer these products.

For more on making your home livable, see *AARP's Home Fit Guide* at aarp.org.

Your Hearing

You may, at some point, suffer some hearing loss. About 30 million Americans suffer from hearing loss in both ears, and the incidence of hearing loss increases with age, according to a 2011

Johns Hopkins study published in *Archives of Internal Medicine.* The American Speech-Language-Hearing Association estimates that a staggering one-third of adults 65 and older face hearing loss. With all the rock music that's been blasted in our ears for so many years, iPods plugged in all the time, and city noise pollution assaulting us constantly, it's a wonder we're not *all* hard of hearing.

Hearing loss has a huge impact on our lives: it basically cuts us off from people. You can literally watch someone tune out of conversations when they get tired of saying, "What?" all the time. Imagine the isolation you would feel. Imagine how easy it would be to just withdraw. Although there is no rational justification for the stigma of being hearing impaired, hearing loss seems to affect people emotionally, and they resist admitting they've suffered a hearing loss. Despite the many well-known people, including President Bill Clinton, who have felt comfortable acknowledging a hearing loss and displaying hearing aids—and given the sympathy we extend to a young person wearing a hearing aid—acceptance of hearing loss by older adults is still stigmatized.

How do you know you are losing your hearing? You can watch for a number of signs: You're often saying, "What?" You ask people to repeat themselves, particularly when there's surrounding noise. The TV never seems loud enough (except perhaps for the commercials, which are often decibels louder than the program content). But the truth is you won't know unless a specialist tests your hearing. If your doctor suspects hearing loss, it's likely you will be referred to an audiologist, a licensed professional who is not a doctor but who can perform a hearing evaluation. If your doctor suspects something more serious than just hearing loss due to aging, you'll likely be referred to an "otolaryngologist," a medical doctor specializing in diseases of the ear.

Types of Hearing Loss   There are two basic types of hearing loss:

1. *Conductive hearing loss* usually involves the outer and middle ear and can result from a blockage of wax, a punctured eardrum, birth defects, or infections. Many conductive hearing losses are correctable through surgery or medical treatment.

2. *Sensorineural hearing loss* is a type of damage to the inner ear caused by age, although it can also be caused by viral and bacterial infections, head trauma, loud noises, medications, and fluid buildup in the inner ear. Rarely can sensorineural hearing loss be corrected surgically or medically. Instead, it is usually treated with hearing aids and other devices.

Tip

The extent of sensorineural hearing loss can vary. Different people lose the ability to hear different pitches or frequencies of sound, not sound in general. In fact, it's quite common for people to lose their ability to hear upper registers as they age, which may explain why you have an easier time hearing a man's voice than a woman's.

People also commonly lose a degree of sound "clarity" in which certain consonants are not distinguishable from each other ("s" and "f," for example, or "b" and "p"). If you have this type of hearing loss, you will be better able to hear if you ask people to speak more clearly and slowly.

Hearing Aids Hearing aids are basically electronic amplifying devices in which small microphones pick up and selectively process sound waves that can be transmitted as signals into the ear through small speakers.

Hearing aids differ in a number of ways. The most important difference involves the type of hearing loss they aim to correct. Just as some stereos are better equipped to pick up some frequencies than others, depending on equalizers and other high-tech equipment they employ, so, too do some hearing aids work better for certain people. That's why it's essential to have an audio specialist evaluate the specific type of hearing loss you are experiencing.

Hearing aids also come in different shapes and sizes. Some are self-contained units that fit snugly into the ear, while others have earpieces connected to larger transmitters. The specific model best suited for you is the one that

- Addresses your specific hearing loss.
- Fits most easily in your ear.
- Has controls you can most easily adjust. (People with limited dexterity may have difficulty adjusting the controls in tiny hearing aids.)
- Addresses your vanity. Some aids are more hidden than others.

Nine Rules for Purchasing Hearing Aids Hearing aids are sold in stores over the counter, by mail order (although that is illegal in some states), and even by door-to-door salespeople who prey upon older folks. To be sure you're getting the best hearing aids for your condition, follow this advice:

1. If the dispenser uses high-pressure sales tactics, it's probably best to find another dispenser.
2. Make sure you get a *written* warranty.
3. Confirm with the dispenser and the manufacturer that they both honor the warranty.
4. Choose a dispenser that offers a trial period for use and charges only a small service fee, if any, for returning the hearing aids within the first 30, 60, or 90 days. (As a rule, dispensers can return hearing aids to most manufacturers within 60 or 90 days for a *complete* refund.) If you purchase hearing aids from a door-to-door salesperson, you have the right, by law, to cancel the order within three business days and get a complete refund, including any deposit.
5. Find out what training and other services the dispenser will provide free of charge, and for how long. In particular, make sure the dispenser will explain how to get accustomed to wearing hearing aids, how to adjust them, and how to eliminate ringing or feedback.
6. Check the reliability of the hearing aid dispenser through the Better Business Bureau, consumer protection agency, or state attorney general's office.
7. Ask for and check the references of the hearing aid dispenser.
8. Be wary of purchasing hearing aids through the mail (and it's illegal in some states). Consider the difficulty of getting

the right fit, correctly adjusting the hearing aids for your needs, and learning how to use them.

9. Choose a dispenser that will loan you hearing aids when yours need to be repaired.

Legal Oversight The Food and Drug Administration (FDA) is responsible for enforcing regulations that deal with the manufacture and sale of hearing aids. According to FDA regulations, all dispensers of hearing aids must meet the following criteria:

- Dispensers of hearing aids must advise patients who have a hearing problem to consult a physician before purchasing a hearing aid.
- Dispensers must obtain a written statement from the patient, signed by a licensed physician and dated within the previous six months. This statement must say that the patient's hearing has been medically evaluated and that the patient is cleared for a hearing aid fitting.
- Although anyone over 18 can sign a waiver for the medical examination requirement, all dispensers must advise the patient that waiving the examination is not in the patient's best health interest and dispensers must avoid encouraging the patient to waive the medical evaluation requirement.
- Dispensers must provide a complete set of instructions for the operation, use, and care of the hearing aids, including a list of sources for repair and maintenance.
- Dispensers must provide a disclaimer that states, "The use of a hearing aid may be only a part of a rehabilitative program."

The Medicine Chest

As we get older, more of us take more medicines daily then ever before, whether for managing high cholesterol, high blood pressure, osteoporosis, blood clots (hence the advice to down a daily dose of baby aspirin), or other conditions. For some of us, the number of pills we take daily is staggering. In part, this pill popping indicates how much our bodies stop working as we age. It's also a sign of the technological and medical advancements that have given us so much knowledge about how our bodies are supposed to work.

There are several problems that spring from this situation:

- The side effects of some drugs are substantial, so much so that medications are frequently prescribed to treat the side effects of the original prescription. This snowball effect causes problems of its own.
- Coordinating the use of myriad drugs is incredibly complicated. Specialists may prescribe a medication without fully understanding or knowing a patient's medical history. So unless you report *every* drug prescribed to a coordinating physician or pharmacist, you could be taking two drugs that cancel each other out.
- Managing the number of pills prescribed can seem like a full-time job: Some of them must be taken with meals, some on an empty stomach, some cannot be taken with juice, some are better with juice, some should be taken with milk to minimize stomach upset, some cannot be taken with milk, some must be taken on alternate days, some two or more times per day, and the specifications go on and on.
- The cost of these pills is mindboggling. While some insurance programs reimburse for medications and Medicare Part D provides some relief, the cost of most medications is not fully covered; either there's a co-payment or the plan covers only a percentage, anywhere from 80 percent to as little as 50 percent. For more information read *Medicare Prescription Drug Coverage for Dummies* by Patricia Barry (John Wiley & Sons, 2008).
- Some prescription medications can be addictive. Even when the addiction is life saving rather than life threatening, you can still become physically dependent.

To see how your prescription drugs, over-the-counter drugs, herbs, and supplements interact with each other and with other substances, see AARP's Drug Interaction Checker at http://healthtools.aarp.org/drug-interactions. To help you find lower-cost, therapeutically similar medications to treat your conditions, see AARP's Drug Savings Tool at www.aarp.org/drugsavings.

Twenty Questions You Should Ask Your Doctor about Prescriptions

1. What is this prescription for?
2. Is there any other way to treat this condition rather than through prescription medication, such as over-the-counter drugs, changes in diet, or increased exercise?
3. Will this drug cause drowsiness?
4. Will this drug cause diarrhea or stomach upset?
5. What are the other potential side effects?
6. Can this drug be taken safely and effectively with my other current medications?
7. How often should I take this medication?
8. For how long should I take it?
9. Should I avoid any over-the-counter medications or abstain from eating certain foods or drinking alcohol while taking this medication?
10. Should I take this medication with meals, with a snack, or on an empty stomach? Does it matter?
11. If with meals, does it matter if it's before, during, or after?
12. Should I take this with water, milk, or juice? Does it matter?
13. What should I do if I forget to take a pill? Take a double dose the next time or just continue with one?
14. Will I feel better after taking this drug? When should I expect to feel better?
15. If I don't feel better, how will I know if it's working?
16. If I have trouble swallowing the pill, can it be broken in half or crushed and put into food?
17. If I have a specific allergy, will it be a problem if I take this drug?
18. What is the allergic reaction to this drug?
19. Is there a generic form of this drug, or must I take the name brand?
20. Does the doctor have any free samples I can have to get started?

To keep track of all your medications, including over-the-counter drugs and herbal supplements, print out and complete a personal medication record at www.aarp.org/medicationrecord. Make sure you bring it with you to your doctors' appointments.

Buying Medication

The cost of prescription drugs can be enormous, even with insurance coverage. There are a number of ways can you save on medication. Here are nine suggestions:

1. If you're eligible for Medicare, check whether you would be better off with private prescription coverage or Medicare Part D. Sometimes, particularly if one medication is fully covered by a private plan but only partially covered by Medicare Part D, it's more cost effective to purchase the private coverage rather than Medicare Part D.
2. Ask the doctor for the generic equivalent or lower-cost brands that are therapeutically equivalent to the name brand.
3. Ask the doctor if you can get a dosage that's twice the strength and then cut the pills in half, effectively cutting the price in half. (Then be sure you don't take the whole pill!) Pill splitters can be purchased in many drug stores.
4. Ask the doctor for free samples of the medication.
5. Check to see whether one of the mail-order prescription services offers a lower price. But be a diligent shopper, since a mail-order house may charge less for some medications while charging more for others.
6. Check to see whether one of the big-box stores (such as BJ's, Costco, or Sam's Club) or major drugstore chains (such as CVS, Target, and Walgreens) sells the drug for less than the co-pay or other charge under an insurance program. Because these stores buy in such large quantities, they can sometimes offer the drug for less.
7. If the medication will be an ongoing prescription, order bulk quantities at one time (if your prescription qualifies and your insurance allows it), which may cost less. If you are responsible for a co-payment, this cuts down on the number of co-payments over time.

8. If this is a new prescription for a medication you took at an earlier date but discontinued, check to see whether you have any pills left from the previous prescription. *But check the expiration date on the vial to be sure the pills are not out of date.*

9. Find out if the manufacturer of the drug offers programs for people with limited incomes.

Choosing a Doctor

Chances are as you age you will at some time have to find and select a new doctor, whether due to illness, a change in residence, the need for a specialist, or a change in your health insurance carrier. It's possible that your current physician does not accept Medicare, and when you turn 65 and enroll, you may need to find a doctor who does.

Doctors differ, just as other professionals (like lawyers and accountants) do: in their knowledge, in their ability to communicate with patients (or clients), and in how diligently they stay abreast of the latest information. Doctors also differ in their points of view: a surgeon may see surgery as the best way to deal with a problem, while an internist may look to medication and other nonsurgical options to handle the situation before recommending a patient "go under the knife." Both may be viable means of treating the condition. But which is the right one, the best one, *for you?*

It's essential that whichever doctor you see knows as much about you as possible. A doctor should know not only your and your immediate family's medical history, but also nonmedical aspects including your lifestyle, personality, and beliefs. Although most doctors understand the importance these factors play in a person's health and recovery, physicians usually do not have the time to learn much about a patient's habits or traits. They must treat the patient, but often that means treating the symptom or the problem, not the whole person. If, for example, you do not respond well to the kind of expert that flies into the exam room, spends a few moments, leaves with barely a few words, and makes crucial decisions for you, tell the doctor that this kind of approach is not acceptable and that you want and need more information.

Note

It's up to *you* to make sure the doctor knows about your other important conditions and medications. When seeing a doctor for the first time, make sure you communicate the intangible parts of your condition as well (such as your worry about the symptom or your concern about a family history). Don't be passive. It's not good for you, and it's not good medicine.

There's no single doctor that's right for you; there are many. Sometimes you may have to balance poor bedside manner with brilliant diagnostics, but the choice should be yours. Here are some ways you can find a doctor you can live with:

- Get recommendations from another doctor. Most know who is good in their field and who should be avoided, although some referrals could be based on social contacts. Request three names and ask which one is the top recommendation. Find out if the referring doctor ever used the recommended doctor or referred family members.
- Get a recommendation from nurses and other medical personnel. Often people who work in hospitals, clinics, and other health-care facilities know how good doctors are and how well they deal with patients. They also know the reputations of doctors, since they are privy to some of the comments doctors make about their peers and colleagues.
- Ask family members and friends. Ask, too, about doctors to avoid and always find out why a person recommends or rejects a doctor.
- Check with a local hospital's doctor referral service.
- Ask your insurance company for a list of participating doctors in your area. You can call the company or search on its website.
- Call a local university medical school and ask to speak to the head of the clinical residency program to get a recommendation.
- Find doctors through referring companies such as these. (Online searches may yield inaccurate results due to errors, subjectivity, or outdated information. Be sure you follow up with a phone call.)

- 1-800-DOCTORS, a private, for-profit company that refers you to doctors who fit your criteria (zip code, insurance program, and "what you're looking for in doctor"). The doctors pay to participate in this service so there is no fee to the caller.
- Doctor Finder, https://extapps.ama-assn.org/doctor finder/home.jsp, supported by the American Medical Association, which provides two lists, AMA members and nonmembers. You can search by doctor name or specialty. Findings list office location, contact number, board certifications and education.
- Healthgrades.com, a free Internet doctor ranking service. You can search by location for doctors, hospitals, and dentists. Findings include information on insurance, malpractice suits, age, and education.

When looking for a doctor, you may find some in a relatively new concept called a "concierge" practice, also known as boutique medicine or direct care, where you pay an annual fee and have greater access because the doctor has many fewer patients. These fees can be quite high, $1,500 or more per individual.

Whatever doctor or type of practice you're looking at, consider these factors:

- Convenience to your home (including available parking or accessibility to public transportation).
- Hours available for appointments.
- Whether the doctor accepts assignment (see discussion of Medicare in Chapter 4, "All About Health Insurance").
- Whether the doctor participates in your health plan.
- Whether the doctor accepts payments directly from your health plan or if you must pay and get reimbursed.
- If the doctor is a specialist, whether he or she is "board-certified" (you can check on that by calling the American Board of Medical Specialties at 1-866-275-2267 or visiting www.fsmb .org/directory_smb.html.
- At which hospital the doctor has staff privileges (partially for convenience but also to see whether the doctor has staff privilege in a major hospital or not).

- Whether the state medical licensing board has ever disciplined the doctor. You can find out by calling 1-866-275-2267 or visiting www.fsmb.org/directory_smb.html.
- Whether the doctor is a member in good standing of the local medical association.
- Whether the doctor will give a free initial office consultation. If not, the fee for about 20 minutes of the doctor's time should be less than $100. An initial consultation is a critical step in ensuring that you are comfortable with this doctor.
- Whether the doctor will give you an estimate of how much specific treatments will cost—whether or not you are covered by insurance.
- Whether the doctor is available for phone calls or e-mails, and general response time.
- Whether and when the doctor is available in emergencies.
- Who covers for the doctor when he or she is away or busy (in which case you may need to ask many of the same questions to the doctor filling in).

Some people also like to ask questions that probe a bit deeper, such as whether the doctor likes being a doctor. If this approach appeals to you, the answers may give you insight into the doctor's attitude toward patients. You might also consider asking about the doctor's philosophy on one of your specific concerns or interests, such as nutrition, second opinions, and managed care health insurance.

Note

Many doctors do not accept new patients. That should be your first question. And if you're on Medicare, be sure to ask whether the doctor is accepting new Medicare patients. You may have to broaden your search to find one or ask colleagues, friends, and even the doctors who declined to take you on. It is a growing problem, particularly in high-cost areas.

Dealing with Depression

Depression is a growing problem with people in their 50s and is generally considered the most widespread mental problem among people over 65. Surveys show that about one-sixth of the 65+ population is depressed, and some experts have estimated that if you include all those who have not been clinically diagnosed with depression, as many as half of those 65+ have experienced depression. Furthermore, there is evidence that the number is growing.

The causes of depression are many and the ramifications are endless. You, or your loved ones, may not even identify symptoms as depression. You may feel sadness or any of the other indications of clinical depression (see below). But it's easy to dismiss an individual symptom, or several at a time, or find logical reasons for them. For example, you may have lost a little weight, not be eating well, and feel "empty" or distressed—normal feelings from time to time. You could easily write them off as reactions to some recent, sad event (like the loss of a friend or relative), or as a side effect of a medication you've started to take, or even to a change in the season. (Winter months, with decreased numbers of daylight hours do, in fact, lead to a form of depression known as Seasonal Affective Disorder.)

But symptoms may indicate that you are clinically depressed. It isn't normal for people old or young to feel depressed all the time. In fact, the majority of older adults feel quite satisfied with their lives. So as a general rule, the U.S. Department of Health and Human Services recommends that if you see three or four of these symptoms over two or more weeks, you should take some action.

The Twelve Symptoms of Clinical Depression

1. Persistent sadness, anxiety, or "empty" mood.
2. Loss of interest or pleasure in ordinary activities, family, or friends.
3. Decreased energy, listlessness, fatigue, feeling "slowed down," especially in the morning.
4. Sleep problems and changes in sleep patterns (such as insomnia, oversleeping, and early morning awakening).
5. Eating problems and changes in eating patterns or foods consumed (also indicated by a loss or gain of appetite or weight).
6. Difficulty concentrating, remembering, or making decisions.
7. Feelings of hopelessness or pessimism.
8. Feelings of guilt, worthlessness, or helplessness.

9. Thoughts of death or suicide.
10. Irritability.
11. Excessive crying.
12. Recurring aches and pains (such as headaches and back-aches) that don't respond to treatment.

Note

If suicidal thoughts cross your mind, or a loved one talks of suicide, *always* take it seriously. Talk to your physician or call the local suicide prevention hotline. You can find the number online at www.suicidehotlines.com, or in your local telephone book, usually in the blue pages or emergency contact section. Talk of suicide may be serious, or it may be just talk. Don't take a gamble; seek help.

Causes of Depression

Clinical depression—the kind of depression that is distinguished from the occasional bout of sadness or "the blues"—can be caused by numerous factors:

Medications: Some medications, including those used to treat high blood pressure and arthritis, list depression as a side effect. Interactions among certain drugs can cause depression, and many older adults take several drugs at once. Make sure your physician knows what drugs you are taking. Don't forget to include over-the-counter (OTC) medications in your list. Often OTC medications are just weaker versions of prescription drugs. They may have the same chemicals, but in different proportions. (See more about medications below.)

Alcohol: Alcoholism and excessive drinking are usually thought of as symptoms, not causes, of depression. But even moderate amounts of alcohol, especially in combination with other medicines, can cause depression. Furthermore, alcohol can cause or increase forgetfulness, confusion, and an ability to concentrate, which can make depression worse.

Physical illness: Illnesses can be either a cause or a symptom of depression. For example, diabetes, strokes, hormonal changes or disorders, Parkinson's disease, and cancer may cause many of the symptoms of depression. Similarly, coping with life-threatening diseases such as cancer and heart disease or physical deterioration (as a result of stroke, or a loss of hearing or vision, for example) may cause depression.

Internal chemical changes: As people age, their body chemistry changes. The reduction or increase of chemicals produced in our bodies may lead to depression. Increased stress may also change body makeup and chemical balance.

Life events: Many external events and lifestyle changes can lead to depression: illness, divorce, or the death of a loved one, family pet, or friend (and the increasing frequency, as old age approaches, of seeing peers die). Financial setbacks bring on depression in older adults, too. Moving from one residence to another or to another geographic location is another highly stressful event, and a leading cause of depression; many older people are forced to move because of finances or physical infirmities. Even positive, highly anticipated, and welcome changes, such as retirement, can cause stress that leads to depression.

Genetic makeup: Some causes of depression are directly linked to genes. For example, it has been shown that people with very low self-esteem for a prolonged period, or those who are very dependent on other people, can trace the disorder to a genetic proclivity.

Treatments for Depression

Depression is often easily treated. In fact, studies estimate that 80 to 90 percent of those treated for depression respond positively. One of the key factors in successful treatment is early intervention. Common treatment includes medication (anti-depressants) and counseling or, more often, a combination of the two.

Your physician will be in a better position to determine how to treat depression than a doctor unfamiliar with your medical history.

Alert your doctor to the signs of depression as you notice them, and communicate lifestyle changes and other stressful events.

Options for counseling are varied and available in most locales today, whether rural or urban, and often provided by psychiatrists or psychologists who specialize in treating depression. There are specialists that focus on geriatrics, too. To find the right professional, turn to the appropriate physician for a referral or check with the local senior center, hospital, or social service agency.

What You Can Do

Early intervention is one of the most effective ways to treat depression. If you or your loved one experience several of the symptoms listed above for more than two weeks, you should ask for help. The following seven pointers can help you managing your physical and mental health care responsibly.

1. When you seek professional guidance, talk openly about the symptoms. Remember that one of the symptoms of depression is the feeling that treatment won't help.
2. Make sure your physician is aware of all your current, regular medications, both prescription and over-the-counter.
3. Make sure your physician knows your medical history so that physical disorders can be determined or ruled out as causes.
4. Take advantage of mental health counseling or therapy if it's recommended. Seek out a professional you'll feel comfortable sharing inner feelings with. Many people resist seeing a counselor. But for the most part, the stigma attached to seeking professional help for depression is a thing of the past.
5. If a professional prescribes medication, take it as directed (refer to the 20 questions about medications listed above, which cover a range of considerations). Be especially watchful when and if you consume alcohol.
6. Pay attention to (and keep track of) any side effects of the medication and report them to your physician.

7. Push yourself to be active and to engage in physical exercise, which can increase the benefits of medications and, by itself, lead to feeling better.

Running Hot and Cold

As we get older, we get cold more easily for a number of reasons. Our blood vessels don't dilate or constrict as well as they used to. We don't have as much fatty tissue as we used to, or hair for insulation. Some of us take medications with side effects that cause us to feel cold. Women going through menopause may suffer from hot flashes but are also more sensitive to cold spells. As a result of these factors, we are more prone to hypothermia, a potentially serious condition characterized in the early stages by listlessness and some confusion, and then spiraling toward drowsiness, slurred speech, and unconsciousness. Prolonged overexposure to cold can be fatal.

You can treat mild hypothermia by going into a warm room, wrapping yourself in sweaters or warm blankets, taking a warm bath, and drinking warm fluids. If the condition persists, make sure you seek medical attention.

Middle-aged and older adults are also subject to hyperthermia, or heat stress, for reasons similar to those causing hypothermia. Hyperthermia will usually start with clammy skin (especially palms) and some sweating (although in older age your sweat glands don't work as well to protect the body from overheating). The progressive symptoms of overheating are heavy sweating, nausea, general weakness, and a rapid heartbeat. (It's also worth pointing out that certain medications, as well as strokes, diabetes, Parkinson's disease, and other disorders, can cause sensory deprivation, i.e., a reduction in the ability to feel certain sensations, which can be a factor in hyperthermia.)

Tip

Heatstroke is life threatening. It is characterized by high body temperature, cramps, diarrhea, breathing difficulty, dry skin with no sweating to help the body cool down, and confusion. Immediately seek emergency medical attention if you experience these symptoms. As a first aid, drink plenty of cool water and try to cool down with cool (not cold) compresses with wet sheets.

Dehydration is related to overheating and characterized by confusion, fatigue, and lightheadedness. As you get older, you are more prone to dehydration because, among other reasons, your kidneys don't work as well as they did when you were younger. As a general rule, you should drink as much water and nonalcoholic beverages as you can (eight glasses per day is the often recommended amount). Drinking too much water poses almost no risk, unless a physician wants you on a restricted fluid intake or if incontinence is a problem.

Conclusion

In this chapter, I reviewed some of the health issues we face as we get older: the challenge of adequate nutrition and weight control; failing eyesight; the strain to hear; senior moments versus dementia; increased sensitivity to heat and cold. As the adage goes, "Getting older is not for the faint of heart."

But many of us, as demonstrated by the level of activity scale, are as active as we've ever been, and perhaps even more so. Some of us who are not as physically active as we once were live as full a life as we ever did and are happier than ever before. We just need to know how to keep healthy and take advantage of advances in medical research and technology that can improve the quality of our lives. So that bum knee you've had for 30 years can now be replaced. Or the sore back that prevents you from doing things you love can be rejuvenated with physical therapy. Seemingly magic pills can lower our bad cholesterol or reduce our blood pressure to protect against heart disease, and help women keep their bones strong to prevent osteoporosis. Still, not all of us can be easily healed, and that can get us down. But there's help for that, too.

Now that we've reviewed some of the health issues we face as we get older, let's turn our attention to health insurance.

All About Health Insurance

■ ■ ■

Most of us have access to health insurance now, and the Affordable Care Act may provide additional opportunities depending on how and when it is implemented. In this chapter, I focus on options, choices, and misconceptions related to these types of health insurance plans:

1. Group and individual private health insurance.
2. Government programs including Medicare, Medicaid, and veterans' benefits.
3. Long-term care insurance.

The goal of health insurance is to defray the out-of-pocket expenses associated with health care—often acute care, received for a short, definitive time period. In this section, I go in depth into several options for coverage.

In my interviews with people for this book, the question of whether to buy long-term care insurance kept coming up. Many of us who have seen our parents or older friends dig deeply into their financial resources to pay for their health care wonder whether buying long-term care insurance is necessary or cost effective. As a result, I spend a great deal of time on long-term care insurance to help you decide if it is appropriate for you.

Group and Individual Private Health Insurance

Most of us are familiar with the health insurance programs currently available. The Affordable Care Act will likely lead to many changes over the next several years.

As it stands, most people not covered by government programs are covered by health insurance through group plans, arranged through employers or other groups. Many employers pay all or a portion of the insurance premiums for employees and their dependents. Some employers extend that benefit to retired workers. You can also get coverage from an insurance company made available by groups such as AARP or other organizations you're a member of. Individual private plans may include the same benefits offered through employers or groups, but generally at a higher price.

Within those plans are a number of options, the two most common being preferred provider organizations (PPOs) and health maintenance organizations (HMOs).

PPOs and some HMOs contract with independent health providers, including doctors, hospitals, therapists, labs, and other medical professionals, to offer services at negotiated rates. PPOs, generally more flexible than HMOs, allow patients to go to any provider they choose. If the provider is part of the PPO network, patients pay a small portion of the fee a provider charges (usually referred to as a co-pay). If the provider is out of network, patients pay a larger proportion. Patients may need to pay a yearly deductible before benefits kick in.

HMOs offer managed care within a particular health-care organization. Patients must be members and generally have to see a primary physician to be eligible to see a specialist. But all of the providers are part of the organization, either as paid staff or as contractors. Co-pays and deductibles may also be required.

How the current insurance law will affect health-care options remains to be seen, but in all likelihood these types of organizations are here to stay. The question will be whether the majority of people get health insurance through their employers or as part of some larger, perhaps statewide or national insurance option.

Government Programs

Disclaimer: Portions of material within this chapter have been originally published in AARP's *Social Security for Dummies* (John Wiley & Sons, 2012). This material is reproduced with permission of John Wiley & Sons, Inc.

Medicare

Medicare is a governmental program created by the U.S. Congress to help pay for the medical care of people who are 65 years old and older or people who have disabilities. Medicare is administered by the federal government's Centers for Medicare and Medicaid Services (CMS) and the Social Security Administration. Payments to health-care providers are made through private insurance companies with whom the government contracts. There are several contractors throughout the country, with different contractors for specific states or regions.

You are eligible for Medicare once you turn 65 and have enough work credits, usually 40, under Social Security. You can also qualify if you are younger and are disabled, if you have been receiving Social Security Disability Insurance (SSDI) for at least 24 months before becoming eligible for Medicare.

For retirement benefits, if you are already receiving Social Security benefits, the Social Security Administration will automatically enroll you in Medicare Parts A and B and send you a Medicare card through the mail two or three months before your 65th birthday. Only people who are not receiving Social Security benefits must apply for Medicare. A rapidly growing number of people who are covered beyond age 65 by health insurance provided by an employer for whom they (or their spouses) are still actively working have the right to delay Part B (which costs a monthly premium) without penalty until the person stops work.

At other times, you can subscribe only at certain times of the year unless there is a change in your status or if your particular plan decides to stop participating in Medicare. Check the Medicare website for details.

There are four parts to Medicare, A through D:

Part A, Hospital Insurance: Basic hospital services, including a semiprivate room, regular nursing care, hospital meals, and certain other hospital services (including medications, lab tests, medical appliances, and medical supplies furnished by the facility). Part A also partially covers stays of up to 100 days in a skilled nursing facility as part of recovery following a problem that required a hospital stay of at least three days. Your doctor must approve nursing-home care as necessary. (Such rehabilitation is not considered long-term care.) Under Part A, you also can receive certain home health-care services, if approved by your doctor.

Part B, Medical Insurance: Covers doctors' services (including surgeons', anesthetists' and any other doctors' care performed in hospitals); outpatient care such as screenings and lab tests; and medical equipment and supplies. It also covers these services for people who have Medicare and live in long-term care facilities. Part B covers 80 percent of the cost of most services, including doctor visits, outpatient care, certain tests conducted outside hospitals, and an assortment of other medical services, including some done inside the hospital, such as surgery. (It pays a smaller share of outpatient mental-health services, although that is scheduled to rise to 80 percent by 2014.) Some preventive services come free of charge. You pay a monthly premium for Part B, with higher-income seniors charged more. The standard Part B premium was set at $104.90 for 2013. Part B also has an annual deductible ($147 in 2013). After you've met the deductible, you typically pay 20 percent of the cost of approved services. Here's a partial list of these services:

- Approved medical services provided by a physician who treats Medicare patients: The treatment can take place in the doctor's office, a hospital, a clinic, or a rehabilitation facility.
- An annual wellness visit and a one-time only preventive checkup within the first year of signing up for Part B: Both of these are free (no deductible or co-pay) if you go to a doctor who accepts the Medicare-approved cost as full reimbursement.

- Preventive screenings, diagnostic tests, and lab tests in clinics and other non-hospital settings, some of which are free.
- Certain emergency-room services and home health services.
- Oxygen equipment, diabetic supplies, braces, wheelchairs, walkers, and other medical equipment.
- Outpatient mental-health services.

Part C, Medicare Advantage (formerly known as Medicare+ Choice): An alternative to traditional Medicare, Medicare Advantage plans under Part C are run by private insurance companies. They must offer all the benefits of traditional Medicare (Parts A and B). But they may charge lower co-pays and offer some additional services, such as routine hearing, vision, and dental care. Most Medicare Advantage plans include Part D (prescription-drug coverage). If you enroll in a Medicare Advantage plan, you deal with a particular healthcare organization and must accept its rules. You're still responsible for paying the Medicare Part B premium, in addition to whatever the Medicare Advantage plan charges you. (Some plans in some areas don't charge an additional premium.) Most Medicare Advantage plans are health maintenance organizations (HMOs) or preferred provider organizations (PPOs) that offer managed care. They may restrict your choice of doctor or charge higher co-pays to see out-of-network providers, except in emergencies. In other words, you may give up some of your freedom to choose your own doctors (which is your right under traditional Medicare).

Medicare Advantage plans set their own fee structure, including deductibles and co-pays. These fees often, but not always, are lower than those charged by traditional Medicare. But by law, Medicare Advantage plans must put an annual limit on out-of-pocket costs. Traditional Medicare does not have an annual cap on costs you may have to pay.

Part D, Medicare Prescription Drug Insurance: This part of Medicare helps pay for prescription medications. Part D is handled by private plans that have been approved by Medicare. These include stand-alone drug plans, as well as broader Medicare Advantage plans that also cover prescription drugs under Part D. To get Medicare drug coverage in a stand-alone plan, you must actively enroll and pay a monthly premium. Medicare Advantage plans that offer Part D coverage include it in their premiums, and some charge no premiums for either medical services or drug coverage. Part D plans vary widely, both in terms of the list of drugs covered (the formulary) and in terms of the premiums. Most premiums are in the range of $35 to $50 per month. Co-pays, even for the same drug, may vary widely among different plans.

Medigap

You may buy private insurance to help cover some or most of your out-of-pocket expenses in traditional Medicare, such as Part B co-pays and hospital deductibles. Such insurance is called Medicare supplemental or Medigap. It comes in different standardized packages, and you pay a premium (on top of your Part B premium).

Some policies cover more than others. Each of the 10 standard packages is labeled with a letter — A, B, C, D, F, G, K, L, M, or N. (The missing letters belonged to Medigap policies that have been eliminated.) The better the coverage, the more you usually have to pay in premiums.

Medicare and Medigap are too complicated a program to cover in a cursory manner in one chapter of a book. For a more thorough treatment, go to www.medicare.gov. Or you can look at AARP's *Social Security for Dummies* (John Wiley & Sons, 2012), AARP's *Medicare for Dummies* (John Wiley & Sons, slated for fall 2013 publication), and AARP's website at www.aarp.org.

Medicaid

Medicaid is a joint federal and state government health-care program for people with low incomes and limited assets. Much of the funding for Medicaid comes from the federal government (with some matching dollars from states), but it is administered at the state level subject to federal rules.

Since Medicaid eligibility requirements differ somewhat in each state, I won't go into the specifics. But to put some perspective on what "low income" means in this context: Single people receiving the maximum amount of Social Security will usually *not* qualify, regardless of the amount of their assets.

Warning

While Medicaid covers 100 percent of all the charges for most doctors' expenses, not all doctors and long-term care facilities accept patients who are on Medicaid.

If you are eligible for Medicaid, you should become familiar with the rules governing the program, specifically with spending down assets to qualify. We'll talk more about this in the long-term care section of this chapter and later on when discussing finances in Chapter 5.

Veterans' Benefits

In 1996, Congress passed the Uniform Benefits Package as part of the Veterans' Health Care Eligibility Reform Act in an attempt to create uniform rules on eligibility and benefits. The law classified veterans into priority groups. If you are a veteran, then where you rank in the priority group will affect your eligibility for medical and long-term care benefits. Veterans can qualify for a range of free or low-cost benefits and care provided by the Veterans Health Administration (the VHA, under the umbrella of the U.S. Department of Veterans Affairs, or VA) and its hospitals.

The VA provides benefits for custodial care provided at home through the Aid & Attendance Special Pension (A&A); eligibility is heavily weighted, however, toward those veterans with limited financial means. If you qualify for the A&A, you will receive it as a pension benefit.

Nursing home benefits, although limited, are available for most veterans with a service-connected condition or a disability that is rated 70 percent or more disabling. All other veterans are eligible on a resource and space-available basis.

Despite the limitations and strict eligibility requirements, if you are a veteran, then it is worth a call to the VA. You should contact the local VA for more information regarding available services.

Long-Term Care Insurance

Long-term care, as used here, refers to assistance that a person with a chronic condition needs to get through the day. The person receiving these services typically suffers either from a chronic illness or disability, that is, a condition that can be managed but not cured. The primary goal of long-term care is *to help the recipient maintain as much independence as possible*; its timeline is indefinite (remember, the primary goal of short-term or acute care is recovery). Long-term care is not restricted to either a hospital or to any other long-term care facility.

Several misconceptions about long-term care exist. Here I outline the four most prevalent misconceptions and explain the reality surrounding each.

Misconception 1: Long-term care is primarily for old people confined to bed in a nursing home

Reality: While nursing home care is certainly an integral piece in the long-term care puzzle, it is not the only piece. Conceivably, long-term care could begin as home care and progress to nursing home care or some other intermediate level of care. The continuum of long-term care is not defined by a specific facility, or a specific type of care, nor does it have a definitive timeline.

Long-term care is the daily care required due to a cognitive impairment or inability to perform basic functions (activities of daily living) as a result of illness, disability, or frailty experienced through the aging process.

Long-term care services include a range of options and levels, and some are geared to caregivers as well:

- *Adult day services* are community-based, daytime programs that offer health care, nutritional, social, and other related services. The program is generally conducted within a protective setting and is usually available to those who are otherwise being cared for by family members. The goal of an adult day program is to allow individuals to remain either in their homes or in the community while it provides family members with relief from the responsibility of providing care.

- *Home care* offers a variety of services either at home or in another residential setting. Home-care services are designed to assist the individual with basic activities, such as bathing, dressing, and toileting, as well as other services needed to maintain the individual in their home, such as help with meal preparation or assisted transportation.

- *Assisted living facilities*, sometimes referred to as residential health-care facilities, provide assistance to older and frail individuals who are not so impaired that they require the services of a skilled nursing home facility. Assisted-living facilities generally provide group meals, housekeeping, linen services, transportation, preventive health services, and help with personal care.

- *Skilled nursing facilities* provide observation, medical care, treatment, and other skilled services under the direct orders of a physician and can provide 24-hour nursing care under the supervision of a registered nurse.

- *Nursing homes* provide help with daily activities. While residents may not need skilled care, the facilities must have nurses on staff.

- *Respite care* provides temporary relief to family members or friends who are acting as caregivers for an older or disabled individual at home. Respite care is often provided by volunteers, home health-care providers, adult day centers, or nursing homes. It enables caregivers to take the timeouts they need to recharge their batteries, run errands, or relieve stress due to their caretaking responsibility.

Note

Long-term care rarely requires skilled medical practitioners. In fact, the vast majority of individuals in nursing homes receive custodial care to assist with personal needs such as bathing, dressing, and eating, although many people with LTC needs also have medical conditions that require care. Individuals without medical training may provide custodial care, although it must be administered and supervised according to a physician's orders.

Misconception 2: It will never happen to me

Reality: About 70 percent of people over 65 will require some form of long-term care at some point in their lives, and more than 40 percent of people will reside in a nursing home for some period of time, according to the National Clearinghouse for Long Term Care Information, U.S. Department of Health and Human Services.

Even more startling is the fact that 40 percent of the people *currently* receiving long-term care are between the ages of 18 and 64!

Misconception 3: I will be able to pay for long-term care expenses out of my own pocket

Reality: Depending upon where you live, the cost for a nursing home varies from $57,000 to more than $232,000 per year, with a national average of about $80,000, according to the Genworth 2012 Cost of Care Survey. This figure does not include all the expenses incurred for care that an individual received prior to being admitted into a nursing home. The key question is this: Based on the funds you have allocated for your retirement income, how many years of long-term care could your nest egg provide?

Annual costs of long-term care, no matter where that care is received, are astronomical and promise to rise over the years. Not many individuals are in a financial position to bear the full brunt of long-term care expenses. Fidelity Investments began tracking 401(k) balances in 1998. As of December 31, 2012, the average 401(k) balance of investors was $77,300—that's the cost of care for approximately one year at some of the nation's least expensive nursing homes. The problem of self-funding becomes self-evident.

The likelihood that you will be able to pay for your long-term care expenses out-of-pocket is slim.

How can we pay for the exorbitant costs of long-term care? There are four options available:

1. Medicaid (the needs-based government-funded health care available to eligible low-income people regardless of age).
2. Veterans Administration (provider of health care and hospitalization for current and prior members of the U.S. armed services).

3. Private funding (from your own or another family member's funds).
4. Long-term care insurance.

Misconception 4: Medicare and Medicaid are the two largest payers of long-term care

Reality: The majority of people who need long-term care receive all their help from family members and friends.

Medicare is designed to provide funding for *acute care*. That is, it pays the expenses for a type of care whose main goal is recovery. Medicare also provides funding for *chronic care*, which is for ongoing health conditions that can be managed, although perhaps not cured. While Medicare does provide some long-term care benefits, they are very limited in scope and they follow fairly restrictive eligibility requirements. In general, Medicare will cover the costs associated with skilled nursing home care for up to 100 days in a benefit period only after a prior hospitalization of three consecutive days. Also, you must be admitted for skilled nursing care within 30 days of your discharge from the hospital, and the nursing home must be a Medicare-approved facility.

In addition, for the most part, Medicare pays only for skilled care. Unfortunately, *skilled care accounts for only 5 percent of nursing home care occupancy, while custodial care represents 95 percent of the care received in a nursing home.* Medicare pays for a limited number of home-care services. Again, these services are limited in their scope and are subject to strict eligibility requirements.

Like Medicare, *Medigap insurance does not cover long-term care expenses.*

Approximately 50 percent of nursing home residents have their costs paid by Medicaid. While the federal government provides most of the funding and regulatory guidance for Medicaid, the individual states largely control the administration of the programs, which vary significantly from state to state. Medicaid is a needs-based program. It bases its calculation on assets, income, and functional need. For the most part, applicants must be impoverished to be eligible to obtain coverage under Medicaid. Medicaid was designed to ensure that health care would always be available for the least fortunate.

For long-term care in the home or community, Medicaid offers *some* benefits but the benefits are limited and the financial eligibility requirements strict. If you are eligible for Medicaid and need home care services beyond skilled care, talk with an adviser in your county's Social Services office to determine what and how much care will be covered.

Is Long-Term Care Insurance Right for You?

Although long-term care insurance is designed specifically to pay for long-term care, the decision to buy it stems from what you can afford and the motive driving any other insurance product purchase: *risk management.*

Most of us have health insurance. Many of us have life insurance. A smaller number of us have long-term disability insurance. We choose to purchase these insurance policies because we are not willing to assume the risk of being without coverage. For some of us, the cost of most of these products is justified since the potential cost of not being covered is enormous. Understanding the consequences of not owning insurance and the financial and emotional toll inflicted on other family members is what really motivates an individual to purchase insurance. Keep in mind, though, that you must be able to afford the premiums, and you usually must pay the premiums until you need care. Premiums vary depending on factors such as benefits, age, location, and health status, but in 2010, the average annual premium paid by individual purchasers was $2,283.

Who is a candidate for long-term care insurance? To prudently plan for long-term care, you need to approach this question just as if you were considering any other insurance product. Remember that each family's circumstance is different, and not all insurance plans may suit yours. Ask yourself the following four questions:

1. Can I, and in the future will I be able to, afford the cost of premiums?
2. Would the economic loss triggered by a tragic event requiring long-term care services deplete everything I own?
3. Is the probability of such an occurrence fairly high?

4. Do I have ample retirement assets and income to pay for all the costs of long-term care?
5. Do I mind reducing my estate if I need long-term care?

If you answered "no" to question 1 and 5, then you may not need or want long-term care insurance.

If you answered "yes" to question 1 and "no" to question 4 and if you are uncomfortable with the prospect of funding long-term care expenses with your own assets, then you may want to consider *transferring the risk* to an insurance company and purchasing long-term care insurance.

If you decide that a long-term care insurance policy may be suitable for you, it's generally best to find a qualified insurance agent, broker, or adviser to assist you in your search for the right carrier and the right policy design.

Choosing the Right Policy

While thousands of insurance companies currently do business in the United States, few of them offer long-term care insurance. So selecting the right insurance carrier and policy becomes a challenge. The selection of the company is important since you are essentially purchasing a promise to pay a claim.

Step 1: Begin the Search First, narrow your search by investigating several insurance carriers. The most important concern as you weigh your options is the company's long-term potential; it has to be around to pay the benefits if and when you need them. Therefore, pick companies with high financial ratings. Four main rating companies exist within the insurance industry: A.M. Best, Duff & Phelps, Moodys, and Standard & Poor's. I prefer A.M. Best, because I find it one of the simplest to decipher. It uses a simple letter grade to rate companies: A++, A+, A, A–, B++, and so on. Usually a safe bet would be to consider companies that are rated no lower than "A" by A.M. Best.

Caveat: Choosing which carriers to include in your search is not an exact science. If you have prior knowledge of a company, by either name recognition, past experience, or referral, include it in your core group.

Examine the size of the company's asset holding and investigate how long it has been in operation, especially in the LTC business. (Many reputable insurance companies have yet to develop a track record in the LTC business.) The company should, upon request, be able to supply you with information regarding its past claims experience. Pay close attention to the history of rate increases. Also, call your state's superintendent of insurance (or a comparable official in your state's Department of Insurance) to see if there are any reported problems with the company or the agent. You can also ask a trusted insurance agent or broker about LTC insurance and the specific companies you've researched. You should make sure the agent is certified and licensed to sell LTC insurance.

Finally, consider companies that offer a variety of policies: individual coverage, joint coverage, family coverage, and partnership plans where applicable. Sometimes it's more cost effective to purchase a joint policy for both you and your spouse, as opposed to two individual policies. Also, combination insurance products (either annuity or life insurance policies that also offer long-term care insurance benefits) have gained more popularity. Individual circumstances will dictate the best route for you. Regardless, the more options the better.

Step 2: Customize the Policy Given the staggering number of variations available today, customizing your policy is the most complicated step in the LTC insurance-purchasing process. In this section I explore key areas of coverage you can tailor to best suit your needs.

Three factors that most influence the cost of your LTC policy:

1. *How much* insurance you purchase, whether you receive either a daily or monthly benefit.
2. *How long* the benefit will last (a period usually defined by a specified number of years).
3. *How soon* the benefit begins (an elimination period defined by a specified number of days).

Following are the benefits offered in long-term care insurance that you must consider when reviewing a plan that's right for you. When considering options, be careful to select only those that are necessary, since options will raise the premium. Also, be careful, when selecting a policy and a company based on price, that you are comparing apples to apples. The policies must cover the same level of care and for the same period of time.

How Much—Daily or Monthly Benefit You may receive policy benefits based on either a daily or monthly option. One is not necessarily better than the other, but a monthly benefit may offer the insured more flexibility. Furthermore, you can choose either an "indemnity" or cash benefit option (which pays the full daily coverage regardless of expenses billed that day), or a traditional "reimbursement of expenses" option (which covers a percentage of daily or monthly benefits up front as soon as you are eligible for benefits). The indemnity option offers the greatest flexibility but also carries the greatest price tag. Not all carriers provide both choices, but several do offer the benefit options in the form of a rider that may be selected for an additional cost. The important thing to remember is that a long-term care benefit may be paid in several ways. Investigate each to determine which best fits your situation.

How Long—The Benefit Period Most benefit periods run 1 to 5 years, and you choose how long you would need benefits. The benefit period you choose will be based on your perception of what the impact would be of extended long-term care versus the cost of the premium. If you have substantial assets and a healthy income stream, then you would be able purchase a longer benefit period. Family history can also play an important role in your decision. For example, if Alzheimer's disease runs in your family, then a longer benefit period may be appropriate, since the condition can last for years.

Benefit amounts and benefit periods work in tandem to provide the insured with a pool of funds. For example, if you purchased a three-year policy that pays $300 per day for nursing home care, the total maximum payout would be $328,500 (365 times $300 times three years). If your care costs only $250 per day, then your coverage would last until your pool of funds was exhausted, or, approximately three years and seven months. This is what is known as *flexible benefits*. This option is important, as your benefits will last longer if you don't use the entire daily or monthly benefit in a given time period.

How Soon—The Elimination Period Typically, insurance carriers offer an elimination period, which is the time between the onset of illness or injury and first benefit payment. The elimination period typically ranges from zero days (immediate) to 90 days. In most cases, you will want to select an elimination period based on two factors: (1) how long you can pay your own way—do you have significant assets that could pay your initial costs, and if so, for how long; and (2) which elimination period provides the most cost-effective coverage. Usually, 60 and 90 days are popular options for elimination periods. Some policies begin counting the days from the time you become disabled; others count only days that you actually pay for services. You will be able to access your policy's benefits sooner if the elimination period counts days of disability toward the elimination period.

Guaranteed Renewability Most LTC insurance policies are guaranteed renewable. That means the insurance company must renew your coverage as long as your premiums are paid on time.

When you purchase a long-term care insurance policy, three scenarios may eventually play out. The first scenario, the most favorable, is that you never use the policy. The second scenario is that you buy the policy and then submit a claim at some point in the future, say 20 years after the initial purchase. With this scenario, you'll want to make sure the policy includes protection against inflation that occurs in the years leading up to when you use the insurance.

The third scenario occurs when you buy a policy and then submit a claim very soon after the issue date, expecting to receive benefits for a number of years. In this scenario, it's important that you own a policy that will adjust the benefit annually to account for increases in the cost of living that result from rising inflation.

Inflation Protection You want the policy to protect the benefit from the eroding effects of inflation after a claim has been submitted. When researching companies, be sure that the company offers a strong cost of living adjustment rider (COLA) rider. There are three broad types of COLA riders that will affect benefits and, of course, the premium: compounding, simple interest, and consumer price index (CPI). Research which will work best for you.

Not all companies offer the same three versions of this rider, so it may be difficult to compare the policies. Inflation riders offer room to compromise coverage in exchange for cost effectiveness (i.e., if owning the compound rider is not in your budget, but you want some type of inflation protection, then you would explore the possibility of purchasing either the simple inflation rider or the CPI rider). Additionally, at certain advanced ages, it may be less appropriate to purchase a COLA rider and more appropriate to purchase a higher initial benefit amount. If you are shopping for long-term care insurance and you are ages 75 or older, then the level of inflation protection may be less critical.

Tip

Because of the complexity of long-term care insurance, I recommend that you enlist the help and guidance of a LTC insurance professional. The cost to you is minimal, and in some cases a professional may not charge any fee other than what's built into the cost of the policy.

Nonforfeiture Benefit   You should purchase a policy only if you intend to continue paying the premiums. But sometimes circumstances change and you may find that you can no longer afford to pay the premium. If you have purchased a nonforfeiture benefit, you will still be entitled to a portion of your benefits if you become disabled. Be aware, though, that buying a nonforfeiture benefit will significantly add to the cost of the policy.

Tip

If you are a caregiver, get duplicate policy statements and bills sent to you to ensure you receive lapse notices. Lapse notices give you a heads-up that something is amiss with the insured's long-term care insurance coverage.

Waiver of Premium Waiver of premium means that if you submit a claim against the policy, the company will waive premiums for a specified time while you are receiving benefits.

Buyer Beware No federal law regulates insurance contracts; each state is left to operate and regulate its own insurance department. Many state commissioners have come together over the years to create homogenous practices and benefits that each individual state may or may not adopt. Many states have adopted uniform benefits and features, especially as they pertain to long-term care partnership policies and tax-qualified long-term care insurance policies. For example, most policies have adopted the same benefit triggers and have defined the same activities of daily living—especially since tax-qualified LTC policies define uniform criteria for triggering policy benefits.

Fifteen Questions to Ask about Long-Term Care Insurance
1. What kind of care is covered?
    a. Skilled nursing care.
    b. Intermediate care.
    c. Custodial care.
    d. Home health care.
2. How much will be paid for each level of care?
3. Is there a waiting period before benefits are payable?
4. How long will the policy pay benefits?
5. Is there a maximum policy benefit?
6. Will benefits increase with inflation?
7. Are pre-existing conditions covered? If so, is there a waiting period?
8. Does the policy impose any eligibility requirements?
    a. Prior hospitalization to receive skilled nursing home benefits.
    b. Need for skilled nursing care prior to payment of custodial care costs.
    c. Prior coverage in a custodial-care facility or hospital to receive home health care.
    d. Coverage only in a Medicare-certified facility.

9. Is Alzheimer's disease or other dementia specifically covered?
10. Can the insurer cancel the policy?
11. Can the premium increase over the life of the policy?
12. Does the policy contain a waiver of premium?
13. Does the insurer have an A rating or better from *Best's Insurance Reports*?
14. Is the insurer experienced in handling health insurance claims?
15. Is the policy guaranteed renewable?

Conclusion

There is no telling what the future holds regarding health insurance in view of the Affordable Care Act. My best guess is that there will be many changes as the years pass.

As insurance coverage changes, you will have to balance and keep up to date on what's best for your family and situation. Employers will need to do the same.

Long-term care insurance is very much a personal decision. No doubt, more and more of us will need assistance as we age. To the extent that you can take care of your later years though insurance or assets you can draw upon, you'll be better off. If one of your goals is to leave a significant portion of your estate to your heirs, you may decide that the risk of losing it all because of failing health may not be worth the risk for you. If you're one of those who say, "My goal is to spend my very last dollars the day I die," then you probably will have a different attitude about health and long-term care insurance. The key is for you to make the decision knowing the facts and through early planning, not when you or a loved one is tossed into a situation where you have to make choices under duress or in isolation.

The largest expenses you'll have as you grow older will likely be for health care and health insurance. Now that I've covered these two areas, in the next chapter I'll focus on your finances.

CHAPTER

Making It Last for the Rest of Your Life

■ ■ ■

At the outset I want to say, emphatically, that money should not be the first thing you think about when deciding how best to live the rest of your life. Still, your choices will be affected by the amount of money you have saved, your income now and in the future, and the ways you choose to spend. So in this chapter, I talk about your finances and about financial strategies to make sure you don't outlive your resources. Specifically, I cover these topics:

1. Getting professional advice.
2. Assessing your Social Security.
3. Creating a financial plan.
4. Evaluating your cash flow and assets, including your home equity.

You probably have spent much time and energy thinking and worrying about your finances, so the material in this chapter will likely supplement what you already know. But if a topic is unfamiliar, you should delve more deeply into it.

A chapter (or even a whole book) can't give you the kind of personalized attention you need. The worksheets can help you crunch numbers and lead you to other useful sources, some of which I provide. But I can't be your financial planner.

What I can do here is give you a basic understanding of how to view your financial situation for the long term and help you define the kind of lifestyle you want to live. I can give you tips and suggestions about ways to maximize what you have. By taking into consideration finances and the other topics I discuss in this book—insurance, health status, legal issues, family relationships, and the level of activity scale—you will be better able to make the key decisions.

Getting Financial Advice

If you don't already work with a professional for financial planning and advice, I encourage you to find one. Professional advice can be invaluable and help steer you toward your goals. While websites and Internet searches can help narrow the search for the kind professional you need, I have found the best way to find the right expert is through personal reference. It's like when you're searching for a good plumber for a major repair: You wouldn't hire someone from the Yellow Pages or Internet without a reference, would you? Your finances and estate are even more critical. Take your time and learn as much as you can about the professional offering the services. And please, *never* pay any money up front.

Tip

Many older Americans are victims of fraud. Many con artists specialize in taking advantage of older people by convincing them that their hard-earned money could be safely making much more than it is. Remember the old adage, "If it sounds too good to be true, it probably is." If you suspect you are being conned, notify the authorities. Also keep in mind that when a major life event occurs—the death of a parent or spouse, or the sale of the family house, for example—you'll be more vulnerable. It's best to not make any major decisions, especially with regard to your finances, until after you have taken a little time to adapt to the major loss or change.

You'll find many types of financial planners and advisers out there. Check credentials carefully; anyone can hang out a shingle.

You may want to consider working with financial planners who hold the CFP® certification, which means they have met education, examination, experience, and ethics requirements. Financial planners will usually cover topics such as these:

- Long- and short-term financial goal setting.
- Evaluation of assets, debt and cash flow.
- Insurance, including health, long-term-care, life, disability, homeowner's, and umbrella policies.
- Investments and savings.
- Retirement planning.
- Estate planning, including wills, trusts, and powers of attorney.

Evaluating Your Social Security

Disclaimer: Portions of material in this section were originally published in AARP's *Social Security for Dummies* by Jonathan Peterson (John Wiley & Sons, 2012). This material is reproduced with permission of John Wiley & Sons, Inc.

We're all familiar with Social Security, and many of us may contribute to it without realizing exactly how it works and how we will benefit from our contributions. Here's a brief explanation. For a thorough treatment of Social Security, see AARP's *Social Security for Dummies*. The Social Security Administration's website at www.ssa.gov also has a wealth of information. Most statistics from this section are from that website.

Your employers withhold (and self-employed individuals pay) taxes to the federal government passed under the Federal Insurance Contributions Act (FICA) for Social Security and Medicare. To qualify for Social Security retirement benefits, you generally must be at least 62 years old. (Note that if you're widowed with no children the age is 60; if you're widowed and disabled the age is 50; if you're widowed with children under 16, there is no age requirement.) There is no means test for Social Security benefits; the amount you receive will depend on the earnings on which you paid Social Security taxes over the years up to a certain limit and the age at which you choose to begin receiving payments.

If you start at age 62, you get a reduced benefit; if you were born before 1955 and you can wait until you're 66, you get the full benefit for which you are eligible. The age for full benefits will gradually increase until it reaches age 67 in the year 2027 for people born in 1960 or later (see Table 5.1). Currently, retirees born between 1943 and 1954 who choose to receive benefits before reaching their full retirement age receive about two-thirds of 1 percent less for each month before their full retirement age. So, at age 62, you'll receive 75 percent of your full benefit; at 63, you'll receive 80 percent; at 64 you'll receive 86.7 percent; and at 65 you'll receive 93.3 percent.

If you're still working and don't need the money to cover your expenses, you may want to delay collecting the Social Security benefit because the extra income generated may increase your average earnings. That means you may qualify for a higher monthly benefit amount at full retirement age. In addition, if you delay retirement past full retirement age, your benefit increases a further 8 percent per year until you reach age 70.

The Social Security tax rate that you and I pay is set by law and is currently 6.2 percent of wages. Employers (and self-employed individuals) pay an additional 6.2 percent, meaning that the Social Security Administration receives a total of 12.4 percent of wages to pay those who are currently receiving Social Security benefits. (Medicare taxes of 1.45 percent are also paid by employers and employees.) The federal government has, in certain years, lowered the individual's contribution to help spur the economy.

Table 5.1   Full Retirement Age Based on Year of Birth

Year of Birth	Full Retirement Age
1943–1954	66
1955	66 and 2 months
1956	66 and 4 months
1957	66 and 6 months
1958	66 and 8 months
1959	66 and 10 months
1960 or later	67

Source: Social Security Administration (www.ssa.gov). This schedule is different for widows and widowers.

How Much Social Security Will You Get?

The amount of monthly retirement benefits you receive depends primarily on the earnings on which you paid Social Security taxes. As a general rule, the benefit is based on average earnings over your lifetime according to the following steps:

1. Your earnings in each year of your career are adjusted for wage inflation.
2. An annual average is found for your top 35 years of wage-inflation-adjusted earnings.
3. A monthly average earnings amount is found by dividing the figure in Step #2 by 12 months.
4. The average adjusted monthly earnings amount is used in a benefit formula specified by law to arrive at your initial monthly benefit amount. Currently, for those who had *average* earnings during their working years, their Social Security benefit will replace about 40 percent of their earnings. For more than average earnings, that percentage will be lower.

You could receive the benefit under this calculation if you wait until the full retirement age to claim your benefits. As described above, your benefit amount may be reduced if you take benefits before your full retirement age. Your benefit amount may also be adjusted if you worked in employment that was not covered by Social Security or if you have earnings and are below the full retirement age.

You can get a detailed analysis of your lifetime earnings and an estimate of the Social Security retirement benefit by requesting a "Personal Earnings and Benefit Estimate Statement" from any Social Security office. You can also get the statement or request one through the Social Security Administration website at www.ssa.gov. Table 5.2 from the Social Security Administration shows examples of Social Security retirement benefits if you retire at your full retirement age and had steady lifetime earnings.

Table 5.2   Examples of Social Security Retirement Benefits (Approximate Monthly Benefits if You Retire at Full Retirement and Had Steady Lifetime Earnings) *(in current dollar values)*

	Current Earnings		
Your Age in 2013	$40,000	$75,000	$120,000
45	$1,353	$2,002	$2,443
55	$1,276	$1,954	$2,370
66	$1,165	$1,786	$2,261

Note: The accuracy of these estimates depends on the pattern of your actual past earnings and on your earnings in the future.

Source: Social Security Administration online calculator, http://www.ssa.gov/oact/quickcalc/index.html.

Take It Now or Later?

One of the key questions you'll have to deal with is whether to take a reduced amount of Social Security before full retirement age or wait until you're eligible for the maximum amount. That's a decision based on a number of factors. Here are the questions you need to ask yourself and the issues you need to weigh:

1. *What's my financial strength now?* If you need the money to live on, by all means start getting what you can as soon as you can. If you don't need it to live on, hold off, since the amount you get by waiting increases every year, even after you reach full retirement age, until you reach age 70. That's probably more than you can earn by taking the money and investing it in safe investments.
2. *Am I still working?* If so, and you earn more than $15,120 per year (the limit in 2013) and you are below the full retirement age, your benefit will be reduced $1 for every $2 you earn over that figure. In the year you reach your

full retirement age, your benefit will be reduced by $1 for every $3 dollars in earnings over $40,080 in 2013, until the month you reach your full retirement age. So it's probably worth holding off until you reach the full retirement age, when there is no income cap on benefits. The annual limit can change every year, so check with the Social Security Administration for updates. Note, though, that you don't actually lose that money. When you reach full retirement age, your benefits will be increased to take into account those months in which you received no benefit or reduced benefits.

3. *Do I have serious health problems? Or more accurately, what's my life expectancy?* The break-even point is about age 78. That means that at age 78, you'll have received about the same cumulative amount whether you started at age 62 with a reduced amount or waited the additional four years. Example: If your full annual benefit is $20,000, for the 12 years between 66 and 78, you'll have received a total of $240,000 (excluding any cost of living increase). If you took the early benefit and received three-quarters of the full eligibility, your annual amount will be $15,000 for 16 years (again, excluding cost of living increases). That comes to exactly the same amount, $240,000. After 78, you do better having waited because your benefit is higher. On the other hand, you had use of the money for those four years, and there's no guarantee you'll reach the age of 78. You can use the very generic life expectancy calculator available from the Social Security Administration at www.socialsecurity. gov/OACT/population/longevity.html or check out www .livingto100.com, a site that calculates an estimated life expectancy based on your answers to various questions about your lifestyle and history.

4. *Am I concerned that Social Security will run out of money?* Social Security can pay full benefits for the next few decades. To learn more about this, see AARP's *Social Security For Dummies.*

Tip

A profitable strategy for some couples is for the higher-income spouse to collect the full benefit at the full retirement age and the other spouse, when reaching the full retirement age, to take the spousal benefit while deferring his or her own. In this way, the spouse deferring will receive almost the same amount while allowing his or her own benefit to grow. This strategy works best when the spouse with the lower benefit defers the benefit and can only be done when both spouses have reached the full retirement age. Talk to your financial adviser about strategies that might be appropriate for you and your spouse depending on your ages and work history.

To apply for benefits, you can either visit one of the Social Security Administration offices throughout the country or call 1-800-772-1213 and ask for an appointment. You will need at least the following (and, if requested, additional documents):

- Social Security card or a record of the number.
- Birth certificate.
- Proof of U.S. citizenship if you were not born in the United States.
- Marriage certificate if you are signing up on a spouse's record.
- Most recent W-2 form, or tax return if you are self-employed.
- Name and account number of the bank account in which the benefits will be deposited. (Benefits are now only deposited electronically, eliminating paper checks.)

Even if you don't have everything on this list, don't delay applying. The SSA can often assist in obtaining certain documents.

The processing of your application will take some time, so if you're counting on receiving your benefits on your sixty-sixth birthday, you need to apply at least two to three months before, but not more than four months, according to the Social Security Administration. In addition, the first deposit will not occur in your birth month but rather in the following month.

Planning for Your Later Years

The steps involved in planning for your later years are different depending on the age at which you start planning, for several reasons:

- The older you are, the fewer years you have to prepare.
- Your income will probably decrease in your later years rather than be on the upswing like it was when you were younger because you will be drawing down your savings and investments, and your pension and other retirement income may not have a cost-of-living adjustment (COLA).
- You cannot afford as much volatility in your investments because you have less time to ride out the lows.
- You will likely need to live off the income your assets generate, or even draw down your assets, rather than continuing to have them grow.
- You must make more provisions for catastrophic illness or emergency.
- You may be less able to manage your money on your own because of failing health or cognitive decline.

Regardless of the differing factors for age, these five basic steps can help you manage your finances:

1. **Assess what you have.** Calculate your balance sheet; add up your assets and subtract your liabilities.
2. **Figure out your expenses.** Determine your monthly costs for at least the next one or two years, although three or four is better. Use the costs you've had for the past year or two and then add 5 percent per year for inflation. (You can adjust this inflation factor as needed, but 5 percent will give you a rough approximation of how your expenses will increase each year. Although the consumer price index or official inflation rate is lower than that, your health expenses are likely to exceed that low rate.) Add in any anticipated expenses for big events such as weddings, new cars, a new home, and the birth of grandchildren. Also add in some potential expenses for home maintenance and repair. For the long term, you may want to anticipate the need to live in

79

a nursing or assisted living facility. Those figures vary greatly by location, but you can get a rough estimate for your area by checking with the National Association of Area Agencies on Aging at www.n4a.org. Don't forget to increase these anticipated costs by about 5 percent per year, too.

3. **Calculate your income.** Add up all your income, including wages, Social Security, retirement plans, dividends, and interest. For Social Security, use an inflation factor of 2.8 percent per year. Base expected income from assets on what these assets have earned in the past.

4. **Determine the shortfall or surplus.** If there's a shortfall between your expenses and your income, determine how much you will need to take from assets to meet your budget. Then extrapolate how many months or years you can continue to reduce assets to meet expenses before those assets are totally depleted. (Remember, too, that reduced assets yield lower earnings).

5. **Learn about other sources of income and benefits.** Explore the range of assistance programs that can reduce the shortfall or increase the surplus. See if you're eligible for needs-based programs such as SNAP, the Supplemental Nutrition Assistance Program; Supplemental Security Income (SSI); and Meals on Wheels. Look into assistance programs, including reduced or free rides for seniors, store and service discounts, life insurance benefits, and Medigap insurance reimbursements. AARP has a QuickLINK tool for researching options at www.benefitscheckup.org.

Financial planners generally suggest that a reasonable amount to withdraw from savings is 4 percent of the total annually. In that way, you don't take too much from principal so you don't outlive your money. That percentage also allows savings to continue to grow or stay even. Although 4 percent is a reasonable estimate, it doesn't take into account the actual inflation rate or your own expenses. Most of all, it doesn't take into account increased health-care costs, which will probably increase at a rate greater than 4 percent. But chances are, as you age, that your expenses will decrease as you become less active, have fully paid for your home, and have no children to put through college.

When creating a budget, it's helpful to separate expenditures into fixed and variable categories. That way you can see more easily which expenses can be reduced and by how much. You can use the cash-flow budget worksheet that follows (see Figure 5.1) for putting together your budget, and the worksheets available on the AARP website at www.aarp.org/money.

Many planners and financial experts say that when figuring out your budget for your later years, you can approximate your need by taking about 80 percent of your current budget. For many, that figure can be low. You may, for instance, use your increased free time to travel or take up new activities. And although you may not contribute to your retirement savings as much (one of the reasons for the reduced budget), you still may contribute some. I personally recommend using the same budget you have now, unless you can demonstrate that your costs will decrease.

For many people, young and old, cash inflow does not match cash outflow. That's one reason credit card use is so popular—it allows people to continue their spending habits and pay off their bills at a later date. A situation like this for younger people, while not financially healthy, can be overcome through increased income (raises, cost of living increases, overtime, second jobs, new jobs, etc.) or through periodic tightening of the belt.

The problem of having a shortfall is more serious as you age because your income is not likely to increase significantly. Social Security will go up at a steady rate (to roughly match inflation, so in real terms it doesn't change much) and dividends and interest will remain relatively constant (and, therefore, may actually lose out to inflation). Furthermore, as you need more money to compensate for a shortfall, and the only place it can come from is your assets, the income realized through investment interest will decrease, causing an even greater shortfall. So the shortfall problem is compounded. "The average savings for retirement is something like $50,000," according to economist Ben Stein, "and a lot of baby boomers have no savings at all for retirement." Yet to maintain their current standard of living after 65, many 50- or 60-year-olds will need to have saved more than $400,000.

Preparing a budget is an excellent way to review your expenditures. You may discover you are paying for things you no longer

BUDGET WORKSHEET

Fixed Expenses

Household: Rent/mortgage   _____
                     Property tax   _____
                     Gardener/lawn and tree service   _____
                     Domestic help   _____

Insurance: Homeowners/renters insurance   _____
                     Life insurance   _____
                     Automobile insurance   _____
                     Health insurance/Medicare premium   _____
                     Medigap insurance premium   _____

Loans: Automobile   _____
                     Other fixed loans or credit   _____

Total Fixed Expenses   _____

Variable Expenses

Household: Utilities (gas, electric, water, sewer)   _____
                     Home repair   _____
                     Telephone   _____
                     Groceries   _____

Medical: Doctors/dentists   _____
                     Therapy   _____
                     Prescriptions   _____
                     Over-the-counter drugs   _____

Clothing: Laundry/cleaning   _____
                     New purchases   _____

Personal Care: Toiletries   _____
                     Haircuts/styling   _____
                     Miscellaneous   _____

Figure 5.1   Budget Worksheet Expenses

Transportation:	Auto licenses and registration	_____
	Auto gas and oil	_____
	Auto repair	_____
	Parking	_____
Personal:	Dining out	_____
	Entertainment	_____
	Gifts	_____
	Subscriptions and books	_____
	Donations	_____
Miscellaneous:	Bank charges	_____
	Investment expenses	_____
	Legal and professional fees	_____
	Taxes	_____
Total Variable Expenses		_____
TOTAL EXPENSES (fixed plus variable)		_____
Fixed Income	Social Security	_____
	Wages	_____
	Dividends	_____
	Certificates of deposit	_____
	Fixed interest-bearing bank accounts	_____
	Loans	_____
	Rental payments	_____
Total Fixed Income		_____
Variable Income	Capital gains/losses	_____
	Variable-interest bank accounts	_____
	Tax refunds	_____
	Gifts	_____
	Other benefits (assign monetary value)	_____
Total Variable Income		_____
TOTAL INCOME (fixed plus variable)		_____

Figure 5.1 (*Continued*)

need or use, like collision insurance on an eight-year-old car or a large life insurance policy.

Assessing Whether You Have Enough

First you have to determine how much cash you will need from your investments to live on. Here's how that's done.

1. Determine how much you need to live on per year.
2. Determine how much fixed income you receive (wages, Social Security, retirement accounts, pensions, annuities, etc.).
3. Determine how much must be realized from investments to meet the remaining need if there's a shortfall.
4. Determine what return on investment is needed to meet your need.

Table 5.3 can help you calculate the amount of your shortfall for expenses. Let's say you need about $40,000 per year to live on and these costs will increase 5 percent per year. (While inflation may only be 3 percent currently, figure that your costs may increase at 5 percent.) If you receive about $18,000 per year from Social Security and $12,000 per year from a retirement plan, the shortfall is $10,000 per year. If your assets are $150,000, then the return would have to be almost 7 percent to make up the shortfall. In the second year your costs would be about $42,000, which means either that the investments would have to earn more or $2,000 would have to be tapped from assets.

For the third year, assuming all the same percentage increases, costs would be $44,100 and the income based on even lower assets. That means you'd either have to get a higher return on investment (an unlikely scenario), or take money from your assets to meet the shortfall. Each year you will need to take more and more from assets, compounded by increased costs and declining assets. If you work out the arithmetic, you'll see that in just 12 years, your assets would be depleted. That means that a 65-year-old person, not working any longer, living off Social Security and pension, with a 5 percent return on $150,000 in invested assets, would be broke at age 77.

Table 5.3   Projected Costs and Shortfall (5% yield)

Year	Costs (+5%/year)	Total Assets	Annual Income from Assets (+5% yield)	Social Security Income (+3%/year)	Shortfall
1	$40,000	$150,000	$7,500	$18,000	$2,500
2	$42,000	$147,500	$7,375	$18,450	$4,085
3	$44,100	$143,415	$7,171	$19,096	$5,833
4	$46,305	$137,582	$6,879	$19,669	$7,757
5	$48,620	$129,825	$6,491	$20,259	$9,870
6	$51,051	$119,955	$5,998	$20,866	$12,187
7	$53,604	$107,768	$5,388	$21,493	$14,723
8	$56,284	$93,045	$4,652	$22,138	$17,494
9	$59,098	$75,551	$3,778	$22,802	$20,518
10	$62,053	$55,033	$2,752	$23,486	$23,815
11	$65,155	$3,815	$191	$24,191	$28,773
12	$68,413	0	0	$24,917	$31,496

Table 5.4   Projected Costs and Shortfall (8% yield)

Year	Costs (+5%/year)	Total Assets	Annual Income (+8% yield)	Social Security Income (+3%/year)	Shortfall
1	$30,000	$100,000	$8,000	$15,000	$7,000
2	$31,500	$93,000	$7,440	$15,450	$8,610
3	$33,075	$84,390	$6,751	$15,913	$10,411
4	$34,729	$73,979	$5,918	$16,390	$12,421
5	$36,465	$61,558	$4,924	$16,882	$14,659
6	$38,288	$46,899	$3,752	$17,389	$17,147
7	$40,203	$29,752	$2,380	$17,911	$19,922
8	$42,213	$9,830	$786	$18,448	$22,979

Table 5.4 presents a scenario with a greater return on investments: a 65-year old with $100,000 in assets that yields 8 percent per year, costs of $30,000 per year, no pension, and income from Social Security. The first year's shortfall would be $7,000. With a 5 percent increase in costs and a 3 percent increase in Social Security

each year, by the eighth year all assets would be depleted. This 65-year-old can only look to be financial secure until age 73, a very frightening prospect.

That is why financial advisers may counsel their older clients to keep some money in equities rather than simply putting all the money in safe but low-yielding certificates of deposit or T-bills (Treasury bills). I have heard of some advisers, for example, say that older people should invest as if they would be holding their port-folio for 15 to 20 years, holding about one-third of their capital in a short-term investment (often a money market mutual fund) and the rest in a long-term growth vehicle (often split between domestic and international stock funds). Of course, safety of principal is one of the most important aspects of investing funds for older people. As I said earlier, as you age you often need additional cash from investments to live on and you have less time to make up for invest-ment losses. You must feel comfortable knowing that your principal is safe. How high the return on the investment is will depend on how comfortable you are with risk and fluctuation in the markets. While you may tolerate a little fluctuation in the value of your port-folio, over the long term, your investments need to grow in order to stay up with spiraling costs and inflation.

Many financial advisers will suggest that their older clients buy an annuity, which is a mechanism through which you get a defined amount based on the amount you invest and the period of time benefits will be paid. The amount you receive can be a steady stream of income (fixed annuity) or can vary based on interest rates (variable annuity). Annuities may convey to another person when you die if your annuity includes that provision, or simply ter-minate. You can select from a number of options when purchasing annuities, each depending on your personal and financial situa-tion. Other advisers recommend against annuities for their clients, so be sure you evaluate the best option for you.

In addition, some advisers might suggest using "target-date" (or "life-cycle") funds in their investment strategies. These are essen-tially mutual funds in which the stock and bond asset allocation of the fund changes as investors get closer to their target date, such as a retirement.

You as an investor have many options, but this book cannot provide you with specific investment advice, only general information. I strongly suggest you consult with a financial adviser to maximize the chances that your money will last for your lifetime.

Taking Required Minimum Withdrawals

When you reach the age of 70½, you are required to begin withdrawing funds from your traditional individual retirement accounts (IRAs) and other tax-deferred retirement accounts such as a 401(k). In addition, you will no longer have the option of rolling the funds you have in one type of retirement account into another. The example below explains why this is important to consider.

At the magic age of 70½, you must take a specific amount— a required minimal withdrawal—that's based on life expectancy tables available from the Internal Revenue Service, published in Publication 590, *Individual Retirement Arrangements*.

The required minimum withdrawal is calculated by dividing the account balance in that IRA at the end of the preceding calendar year by the life expectancy factor. If you will be turning 70½ in 2013, you would use the balance in the IRA as of December 31, 2011. The IRS life expectancy factor for a 71-year-old single person is 16.3 years, so if you had $265,000 in your IRA as of December 31, 2011, by your 71st birthday, you would have to have withdrawn a minimum of $10,000 in that year. This gets a bit confusing when you cross calendar and tax years, but the general notion is that IRAs and retirement accounts cannot be used to store funds indefinitely. The worksheets and examples in the IRS publication can guide you as you calculate the amount of your required minimum withdrawal.

Withdrawals from retirement accounts are taxable, so you will have to claim the withdrawal amount as regular income (not capital gains). If you withdraw funds from your 401(k) or 403(b), the organization is required to withhold state and federal taxes. IRA withdrawals, on the other hand, while still taxable, are not subject to withholding, so if you have funds in both IRAs and 401(k)s and prefer not to have taxes withheld, you can roll funds from your 401(k) to an IRA.

When Your Home Is Your Asset

Many people have the bulk of their net worth tied up in their home, according to the Center for Retirement Research. If you've lived in that home for some time and diligently paid the mortgage for 25 or 30 years, you may now (or soon) own it outright. Clearly, the equity in your home is available only if you sell the home or borrow against it. And without including the net worth of the home, you may not have enough available capital to produce the amount of income needed to preserve the quality of life you've grown accustomed to.

If you are in this situation, you might want to think about these options:

1. *Sell the home.* Consider moving to smaller living quarters, a less-expensive area, or an established community that costs less. Whether you decide to rent or own, consider these factors:

   - Fewer or smaller rooms.
   - Less maintenance.
   - One-floor living.
   - Warmer climate.
   - Additional or more convenient services.
   - An accessible location for family and friends.

   If selling is an option, you may generate significant resources with which to invest, assuming your home is worth more than what you owe, and after closing costs and any taxes on capital gains. Unless you're used to managing large sums, you should work with a financial adviser to make sure your money is invested appropriately and you are maintaining a well-balanced portfolio. Since the main reason you are selling the home is to be able to live off the proceeds, you should make sure the money is working for you as well as possible.

2. *Refinance the home.* Home equity loans or lines of credit are very attractive options for many people. The interest paid on the loan is usually tax deductible and the interest rates are quite favorable. Home equity loans cost almost nothing

to obtain (usually there is no application fee, although some lenders charge an appraisal fee of a few hundred dollars). With a line of credit, you borrow only what you need, up to a limit. If you've owned your home for a while, chances are the value has appreciated significantly beyond what you paid for it, even with the recent housing crisis. Borrowing against the increase is an excellent way to realize the gain without selling the home and without paying any tax on the gain. Unfortunately, if you are no longer working, you may have trouble qualifying for a home equity line of credit because you have no visible means of repaying the loan except what you receive in Social Security, pension, and investments.

Sometimes lenders will allow you to use scheduled withdrawals from your IRAs and 401(k)s to qualify for a loan.

3. *Reverse mortgages.* Available to homeowners age 62 or older, a reverse mortgage is a loan that enables you to tap your home equity without having to sell your home or make loan payments for as long as you live in the home. Most reverse mortgage loans are federally guaranteed by the Federal Housing Administration's Home Equity Conversion Mortgage Program (HECM).

With a regular mortgage, you make monthly payments to the lender and use your income to repay the debt, which builds up equity in your home. But with a reverse mortgage, you receive money from the lender. So over time, your debt increases and your home equity decreases. You can receive loan proceeds as a lump sum, monthly amount, or as a line of credit where you access funds as needed. The amount of money you can borrow depends on the age of the youngest borrower, the value of the home, current interest rates, upfront costs, and current HECM loan limits. You retain ownership of your home and upon your death, the home passes to your heirs.

You must continue to pay property taxes, homeowner's insurance, homeowner's association dues, and assessments, and you must keep the property maintained. The home must also be your primary residence.

A reverse mortgage becomes due and payable when the last borrower dies or moves out of the home permanently. At that point the loan balance will have grown and your equity may be very small. If you had the loan for a long time, or if your home's value decreased, there may be no equity left. Note that these loans are non-recourse loans, which means that you or your heirs will never owe more than the home is worth. The loan must be repaid when it becomes due, so you or your heirs must pay off the reverse mortgage, sell the home, or turn the home over to the lender.

To obtain a reverse mortgage you must meet with a HUD-certified housing counselor who will explain how the loan works, help you consider other possible options, and answer any questions you might have.

Other Sources of Funds

1. *Loans against retirement accounts.* Some supplemental or optional retirement accounts offer the opportunity to borrow against the value of the account, often at low interest rates and with little or no cost to the borrower. The borrowing limit is generally $50,000 or 80 percent of the value, whichever is lower, and the proceeds of the loan are forwarded within a few weeks of the application. The application itself is quite easy to complete and requires no proof of ability to repay the loan (since you are borrowing from your own money). A retirement account loan can be a means of obtaining funds when emergencies arise. But it should be for emergency use. The money in the account was meant to fund your retirement years. Taking it all out now (and paying more than it's earning) will affect your balance in later years.

2. *Loans against life insurance policies.* Similarly, life insurance policies in which equity is built up through regular payments, such as a universal life policy, offer the opportunity to borrow against the equity. This kind of loan is a potential source of emergency money but, like loans against your retirement account, it should be used cautiously. The purpose of the insurance policy was to protect the surviving spouse or heirs. Using the funds will deplete the protection.

3. *Family loans.* A loan from a family member is a common way to meet expenses. These loans offer many benefits to both parties, but there are also a few disadvantages worth mentioning. On the positive side, if the loan is from a parent to a child, the loan may be somewhat of an "advance" on an inheritance the child will receive. Another benefit to the borrower is that the funds will be offered at low or no interest rates. This means, of course, a lower payback when the loan comes due (perhaps after the parent dies). On the negative side, doing business with relatives can be risky, both emotionally and financially. While I don't necessarily advise against this strategy, I want to make it very clear that loaning money to a relative is a business venture with the potential to cause serious problems in family relationships. Be sure all the terms are spelled out clearly. If you are considering borrowing money from or lending money to your adult child, make sure you fill out loan papers (preferably drawn up by an attorney). Family lenders or borrowers might also consider loaning money against the home equity, rather than just a signature loan. First, that means the loan is collateralized (with the home as collateral and the lender, then, more assured of getting repaid). Second, any interest payments made would probably be tax deductible. Private home equity loans like these should be well documented, particularly if a tax benefit is taken. The IRS has strict rules about the deductibility of family loans (for example, they must be offered at an interest rate at least equal to the "applicable federal rate"), so you should probably seek the advice of a tax adviser. The applicable federal rate can be looked up at the IRS website, www.irs.gov, and is also listed in newspapers.

4. *Gifts.* Tax rules stipulate that any individual can make a gift up to a specific amount ($13,000 in 2012) to any other person without any taxable gain. That means, for example, that if you need funds and your children can afford it, they can each give to you and your spouse $13,000 per year without your having to claim that amount as income on a tax return. (This same concept can be used if you're caring for an aging parent or as a financial planning tool for disbursing your

assets.) A gift is a gift, and that means no one should expect any financial payback. If there is any expectation of being paid back, you should probably consider a family loan as discussed earlier. Again, make sure everything is documented in case either the IRS or a potential heir comes calling.

5. *Viatical settlements.* Under the terms of these programs, terminally ill patients can sell their life insurance policy to a viatical settlement company and receive a lump sum benefit on which to live. If your life expectancy is six months or less, a viatical settlement company will pay up to 80 percent of the face value of the policy; if your life expectancy is two years or less, up to 60 percent. Most companies will require that the insurance policy be in force for at least two years and that the beneficiary of the policy provide a waiver. It is a complex, legal transaction and usually involves a great deal of documentation from physicians. If you are considering this income source, check that the viatical settlement company is licensed by the state and has no complaints against it. Some viatical settlement companies are large enough to have the cash on hand, others are small and get private investors as needed. When working out the details of the settlement, make sure the company either has the cash on hand or already has the investor. Insist on having an escrow account set up so you are assured of timely payments. Be sure you know the potential tax consequences of this program. The payout may be considered a capital gain, and tax laws concerning viatical settlements vary from state to state. Also, if you are receiving public assistance (Medicaid or Supplemental Security Income), check with the Department of Social Services in your state to make sure receiving this payout won't affect your eligibility for assistance. For more information on viatical settlements, contact the U.S. Federal Trade Commission, Box P-Room 403, Washington, DC 20580. You can also access information on the Internet at www.ftc.gov.

Tips for Making It Last

None of us wants to outlive our financial resources. Beyond calculating how much you will take in, creating budgets, and determining how much you'll need to accumulate, consider these strategies to make your money last:

- *Credit:* If you are married, each of you should establish credit in your own name so that when one of you dies, the surviving spouse has a credit history. If you have only joint accounts, or if all credit is in your name, after you die, your spouse may not be able to establish credit in his or her name. That means not being able to even get a credit card.
- *Credit cards:* Don't rack up credit card debt. Pay off your balance each month, and choose a credit card that charges no annual fee. (Several magazines and newspapers publish lists or you can search on the Internet.) There's no reason to pay a fee when you can get the same service for free. Also consider credit cards that pay you back or give you reward points or frequent flyer miles. If you must carry a balance (which, with such high interest rates, is not a good idea for anyone), you'll want to choose a card that offers a low annual percentage rate.
- *Affinity cards:* Airlines, hotels, some stores, and other companies offer rewards for each dollar charged. Using these is an excellent way to accumulate free flights, hotel stays, merchandise, or cash back. Often, you can get a sign-up bonus equivalent to a free flight or several nights in a hotel room.
- *Senior discounts:* Many organizations, including AARP, offer reduced rates for seniors, whether it's a discounted movie ticket, an early-bird dinner, free banking, or special airline fares. If you travel frequently, especially if you visit family often or have a second home, check with the airline or your travel agent to get more information about these programs.
- *Converting IRAs to Roth IRAs:* Investments in traditional IRAs earn money that is tax deferred, that is, you don't pay any

income tax on the earnings until you withdraw the funds. As a result, savings increase more quickly. With Roth IRAs, the main difference is that when you withdraw funds, you do not pay income tax because, unlike traditional IRAs, you have already paid taxes on that deposit. A strategy that many people use is to convert their traditional IRAs to Roth IRAs so that when you withdraw the funds, you don't have to pay taxes on it. However, when you convert to Roth, you are liable for the income tax. You should consult with a tax professional before considering this strategy to make certain it is a smart move for you.

Conclusion

In this chapter I gave you a primer on financial planning while also encouraging you to seek professional assistance. The threat of outliving your money is very real. With the huge decrease in people's net worth as a result of the recent recession, coupled with a decrease in savings rates, more and more people are just an injury or illness away from severe poverty or tragedy. So it's even more important that you go through your budget and crunch the numbers. It's tedious and frightening because we cannot predict the future. But until we see it in black and white—or perhaps black and *red* is a better way to describe it—we won't know our limits.

I'm not a doomsday-ist by any means. I am, in fact, quite optimistic about the future. I urge you, to the extent that you can, to anticipate problems and prepare for them, and then you will be ahead of the game. You picked up this book because you don't want to be a victim. Continue on that path and you'll sleep better at night knowing you've done what you could to prepare yourself and your family for the rest of your life.

In the next chapter, I'll talk about what most of the people I interviewed for this book told me was the scariest part about getting older: "What will my life be like when I'm no longer working full time?"

CHAPTER **6**

Transitioning from Full-Time Work

■ ■ ■

Some life events are almost universally significant: starting kindergarten; graduating from high school; leaving home for college or some other endeavor; graduating from college; starting your first job; becoming eligible for Medicare and Social Security benefits; and leaving the full-time workforce. For some, leaving your full-time job may coincide with eligibility for Social Security; for many, it will occur much later or not at all. In fact, almost three-quarters of Americans expect to work after retirement, according to a 2012 AARP poll.

Regardless of when or why you leave your full-time career, it's definitely a significant transition in your life. And it's a transition for which you cannot be completely prepared, even if you have taken all the financial steps you thought necessary. The feelings that pop up when your life takes you into a new zone are difficult to predict and unique to each of us. This chapter is designed to help you navigate this time by discussing various aspects of retirement:

- Solutions for living on a reduced income.
- How to address the reasons for leaving full-time work.
- Loss of identity.
- Change or loss of workplace friends.

- Social isolation.
- Effect on family and friends.
- Concerns when your partner works and you don't.
- Concerns when you work and your partner doesn't.

Living on a Reduced Income

One of the biggest changes you may face as you step away from working full time will be the reduced income. Presumably, if the choice to leave your job was yours, you've prepared financially for the long term along the lines of what I discussed in the Chapter 5. But often when people first leave their job, they are not fully prepared for the immediate reduction in income. They react in one of two ways: Either they eat out as often, shop as often, and basically live the same lifestyle, or they do the exact opposite and start living as if they are poverty stricken.

The key here is balance, certainly, but mostly planning and analysis. So if you haven't already done so, prepare a budget. It's a fairly tedious task that most people resist, but this is a budget for information purposes only, not an attempt to limit your spending. So I'm going to take a little different approach here than I took in Chapter 5.

Most financial experts suggest breaking up your expenses into two categories—fixed and variable—as I did in Chapter 5 when discussing long-term financial planning. But for this exercise, I think it's more helpful to separate your expenditures into two other categories: mandatory and discretionary. Here's my reasoning: This is not a diet to get you to live within your means; it's more about how you want to live and the way you can maintain consistency in your lifestyle. Until you do this calculation, you won't know if that's even possible. Here's how I would break down expenses in both categories. Use last year's totals unless there's been a significant change.

1. Mandatory:
   - ☐ Mortgage or rent, property taxes, and home insurance (including for second homes).
   - ☐ Home repair (but not home improvements).
   - ☐ Homeowners association dues/condo fees.

- ☐ Medical insurance premiums.
- ☐ Medicines and other medical expenses, including co-pays.
- ☐ Auto insurance premiums.
- ☐ Auto repair.
- ☐ Life insurance premiums.
- ☐ Utilities.
- ☐ Gas and public transportation.
- ☐ Groceries.
- ☐ Telephone, television, and computer.
- ☐ Loan payments (student loans, auto loans, credit card minimums).
- ☐ Child care (if your nest is not yet empty).
- ☐ Bank charges.
- ☐ Investment expenses.
- ☐ Health club or gym dues (if contractual).
- ☐ Haircuts.

2. Discretionary:
   - ☐ Home improvements.
   - ☐ Health club or gym dues (if not contractual).
   - ☐ Dry cleaning.
   - ☐ New clothes.
   - ☐ Gifts.
   - ☐ Donations.
   - ☐ Eating out.
   - ☐ Entertainment.
   - ☐ Domestic help.
   - ☐ Gardner or lawn service.
   - ☐ Vacation expenses.
   - ☐ New purchases of anything not in the mandatory category.
   - ☐ Voluntary contributions to retirement.
   - ☐ Subscriptions (magazines, movies, etc.).

As you can see, the list of mandatory expenses is longer than the list of those things you can cut back on. That doesn't give you as much flexibility as you may want. When you total your expenses and deduct your net income, you will likely see a deficit. That difference is what you'll have to draw from your savings if you choose to live as you have or as you want.

The point of this exercise is to help you get a realistic view of what your life will be like when you cut back your hours or leave full-time work. How much will your daily routine have to change? And, equally important, how much will you have to pull from savings to maintain the lifestyle you want?

Tip

You won't know what it's like or whether you'll be able to manage living on a reduced income until you do it. That kind of experiment could lead to disaster, or it could be a useful learning experience. People have taken the advice of some financial planners and, while still working a full-time job, limited their expenditures for a year or more to what they would be if living on a reduced income. Go ahead and try it if you like. You may find out that it's easier than you thought. Or you may discover early on that you're just not ready for that kind of change.

Addressing the Reason You Left Your Job

The reason you are no longer working full time is important to consider when you're figuring out ways of dealing with the change. By "reason" I mean whether the choice was yours or not. In this section, I am referring to financial issues, health insurance, and social aspects of your life—things to ease the transition for you and your family.

If you have been laid off, fired, downsized, "riffed" (forced out because of a reduction in force), or any other euphemism for having to leave your job without choosing to, you will probably need to deal with a number of concerns. The first, of course, is financial. You will no longer receive your wages, which could cause worry and hardship for you and your family. But unless you were fired "for cause," you will likely be eligible for unemployment insurance benefits, which will pay you somewhere around $400 per week, more or less depending on which state you live in. Although that's not a huge sum, it will help a great deal. You need to register with your state's employment office and follow the directions for claiming benefits. You typically will receive about six months' worth of benefits. If you leave on your own accord, that is if you quit or retire, then you are generally not eligible for unemployment benefits.

You'll also have to deal with health insurance, since most people have insurance through their employers. Regardless of whether you leave your job by choice or through your employer's choice, you can maintain the same health insurance you had when you were working, at least for a period of time. (If you retire, you may be placed in a retirement pool and be able to keep your current health insurance plan indefinitely.)

If you didn't voluntarily quit or retire, your plan will cover you only during a severance period. After that period, eligibility for the insurance plan will be under the Consolidated Omnibus Budget Reconciliation Act of 1985 (COBRA). You and your family may keep your benefits under COBRA for up to 18 months (29 months if you are or become disabled during the first 60 days of COBRA coverage). But during that period, you will have to pay for all of the benefits out of your own pocket. It's possible that you may decide to find an alternative health-care plan, either through a new employer or another group plan. With the new Affordable Health Care Act going into effect in increments over the next several years, you will likely have new possibilities.

When you're no longer working full time, you'll also need to plan for the immediate future. If you chose to leave, then presumably

Life Story

Marty and Carol were both covered under Marty's health insurance plan through his employer. When Marty turned 65, his employer required that Medicare be his primary insurer. Carol was not yet 65, so her employer's insurance plan was still her primary insurer. But because Medicare does not offer dental insurance, both Marty and Carol were covered under her employer's dental plan. When Carol was let go from her job, she could have maintained her dental insurance through COBRA. But without any subsidy from her employer, the plan was more expensive than the coverage she was able to get through another group dental insurance program.

you did so after calculating that it wouldn't cause a financial hardship, and after determining how you would handle the loss in income and any change in insurance coverage. In addition, you probably made some kind of plan for what you would do immediately after leaving the job, such as take a vacation, visit friends and relatives, or pursue a new interest. Or, you might have decided to start a small business or consulting practice.

But if leaving was not your idea, you are now thrust into that searching mode without having had any time to contemplate being unemployed and what that means for your immediate future. The social aspects of leaving a job are usually significant for most people, especially if it was not your choice to leave. If you were fired, you will no doubt have to deal with the reason(s) you were fired. That can certainly take an emotional toll on you and on your family. It can also affect getting a new job, if that's the path you choose.

Once you have dealt with the loss of income (or reduced income if you are eligible for unemployment benefits), your next step will be to determine whether you want to find another full-time job, work part time, totally retire, or take some time before making that decision. The reason you are no longer working will certainly have an effect on your future plans.

Tip

Most career counselors recommend that when you are let go from a job, you take a little time to think about what you want to do, not just jump into the first opportunity that comes along. They also suggest, however, that you not take too long so you don't have to explain in a job application any prolonged absence.

But in a difficult economy like the one we're experiencing now, having a job, even one that's not ideal, may be a lot better than continuing to look.

Confronting the Loss of Identity

Imagine yourself going to a cocktail party at which you know only a few people. As you chat with those around you, one of the first questions will likely be, "So, what do you do?" How will you answer?

If you lost your job but are still planning to stay in your profession, you have a built-in reply, that is, you are "between jobs" or "looking for new opportunities." If you retired, you are likely going to proudly announce that you are retired. But if you are no longer working in your career and have no intention of going back to that field, you may not have an answer that will satisfy you. That loss of identity—to some degree, the measure of who you have always been and how others have perceived you—can be difficult to manage. Some people feel this loss of identity more acutely than others.

So what will you say? How about, "I left my job as a (fill in the blank) and am taking some time to figure out what's next? What do *you* do?" When the subject comes back to you—if it ever does—and you feel comfortable with this person, you might use this opportunity to quiz that person about an interest he or she expressed that is unfamiliar to you. Or you can always steer the conversation toward something that the two of you have in common—if nothing else, the common denominator that brought the two of you to this event.

But the point is, those conversations will happen, and will likely happen often. You need to be prepared for them so you are not thrown into feeling upset about having lost your job and that part of your identity.

Tip

If you lost your job and don't have too much of an idea of what you want to do next, let your imagination wander. When asked, "What do you do?" you can try on a new situation for size by saying, "I *was* a (fill in the blank) but have left that and now I'm thinking about going into (fill in the blank)." It's a great conversation starter, and you may even change what you say periodically. Just let yourself answer with whatever pops up, more or less on whim. By listening to what you say, you may just stumble onto a new and attractive opportunity.

Coping with the Change or Loss of Workplace Friends

For many of us, work life overlaps with social life. We often form close friendships with our colleagues and get together socially, often because we have a common thread between us. When we get together with these friends and colleagues, inevitably there is a little "shop talk," even though we try to avoid it. If nothing else, we talk about people with whom we work.

When you leave that work environment, you no longer have that connection. And for some, the friendship will wane. That's not to say that the friendship wasn't built on a solid foundation; it's just that you no longer have the same focus or common ground. Your conversations will have to take on a new tilt and you'll have to rediscover the connections you have that enhanced the friendship in the first place. Rarely does the shared workplace alone form the friendship. There are many other co-workers with whom you didn't become friends. So the key is to look a bit further (and hope your work friends will do the same) to see what made your relationship closer than others.

Someone you were close with when you worked together may quickly fade from your life. Despite repeated attempts to maintain the friendship—even from both sides—sometimes without that workplace bond, you can't sustain what you had. It can be a bit disheartening when you realize that no amount of effort will be enough. At that point, it's healthy to move on to other friends with whom your relationship can grow based on something other than your work. If you change jobs, even to a part-time position, you'll have a new opportunity to form friendships. Community-based activities or special-interest-based groups, fitness or sports centers, and volunteer organizations also provide new chances to make friends.

Overcoming Social Isolation

I've learned—based on personal experience and on conversations with friends and colleagues—that one of the biggest challenges you will face when you leave your full-time job is the lack of people with whom you interact. At work, you probably had lots of folks to chat with, sometimes meaningfully, sometimes just casually in water-cooler-type conversations about sports or your kids. You may have commuted together. These colleagues perhaps weren't great friends, but there were many people around. You may have had lunches with co-workers or meetings where you were part of a group.

When you leave the full-time work environment, or if you start to work for yourself, you may find yourself having conversations with no one other than a store clerk. If you have a partner who is still working outside the home, this is especially a concern because your only contact will be when he or she comes home tired from a day perhaps surrounded and stimulated by co-workers. In my conversations with people who retired or left employment, this kind of isolation came up often as one of the most difficult things to deal with. It's also a common theme with people who work at home by themselves.

The key to not feeling isolated is, of course, to make an effort to be with people.

Suggestions for Preventing Social Isolation

- Call friends or colleagues on a regular basis.
- Schedule periodic lunches and before-work or late-afternoon get-togethers.
- Join a club that meets regularly.
- Get involved with a community group or other leisure-time activities that involve other people.
- Volunteer for an organization you support.

The Effects of Your Change on Family and Friends

As I implied in the discussion about loss of identity, when you leave your full-time job you are leaving a lifestyle, not just a job. Your family and friends all have viewed you as a doctor/teacher/ accountant/contractor, just as you have viewed yourself that way. But now, you're no longer who you were. You're no longer that professional or that worker. You're someone new and different. "Different" is not something most people are comfortable with, even those closest to you. They may say how much they respect you for having reinvented yourself. But the fact is they will now have to relate to you on a different level.

How you deal with your own identity issue will affect how your family and friends deal with it. If you were unhappily laid off and are feeling lost and upset, then clearly your family will feel that pain. If you left on your own and are joyously living your daily life, there will likely be a big difference in how your friends treat you (but do see the earlier discussion about workplace friends with whom you were close colleagues).

Essentially, you will be forming new relationships with all those people you still consider friends. It's an odd feeling for sure. And for many it can be uncomfortable. But it's also one that can be overcome through communication and trust.

Life Story

In her years as a school principal, Joanna worked long hours at her job, enjoyed few outside interests, and had only a few friends with whom she would get together occasionally. After a long day at work, a lot of her leisure time was spent watching TV or reading before she'd need to get to bed early for the next workday. Even get-togethers with family and friends had to be timed so she could get home early, especially on a school night. Her grown children worried that when their mother retired, she would just do nothing all day and become a hermit. Joanna worried about the same thing. Everyone around her knew her as a busy professional, but now she would be retired. She knew she would have to learn to be by herself more, accept that she was no longer a principal, and begin to relate to the world in this new role.

Indeed, she has done that. She visits with her family and friends more—including on "school nights." She takes trips, including major vacations overseas. TV has become a pastime she rarely has time for since she began volunteering for two different organizations. She has met new people who know her as an active retired person who travels a lot (and wishes she had more time to read).

When Your Partner Works (and You Don't)

Many of our peers have experienced the "empty-nest syndrome," which occurs when the youngest of our children grows up, goes off to school, and finally leaves our home. There's usually a transition period, and many of us have had difficulties with it. It's a bittersweet time. On one hand we're proud of our kids and happy that they've grown up and can make it on their own. On the other hand, we're sad to see them leave and know our relationship will never be the same. But we deal with it, and for the most part learn to adapt to a new life with our partner.

Similarly, when you leave your full-time job, be aware that your life with your partner will never be the same. You are no longer defined by a job—now you're going to be someone new. You'll do different things during the daytime than you used to, you'll be home more, and you'll have new interests. Your work friends and colleagues will no longer be as important in your life as they were, and you may make new friends as you get involved in new activities. Those friends will likely have different interests than the people with whom you shared many of your days.

Your partner, however, may not be undergoing the same transition. What will that do to your relationship? How will things change? When your partner comes home from work, will you be there? Will you be expected to take on more responsibility for running the household? Will you spend the day with no human contact (other than store clerks) and therefore crave conversation? Will you want to do things in your evenings when after working a full day your partner will not? Will your volunteer activities mean you're not at home as much in the evenings?

The questions seem daunting and the solutions are not pat. The key to working out this new relationship is, of course, ongoing communication. You're both going through a transition and you'll both need time to get to know what your new lives will be like. The more you are aware that this is a big change for both of you, the more likely you'll be able to work out the arrangements that will keep you both satisfied.

When You Work (and Your Partner Doesn't)

This is the flip side of the previous issue, but the concerns are the same. How will you feel trudging off to work while your partner lolls about reading the paper and drinking coffee? Will you have different expectations of who's responsible for household chores? If he has new interests through different activities or volunteer work, will you be sharing in those interests? And if she is making new friends through these new activities will you be accepting of these new relationships?

The point of this concern about who works and who doesn't is to realize that over the years, you and your partner have settled into a way of life. You've grown comfortable with the lifestyle, the schedule, and the shared interests. Now one of you is changing that paradigm and throwing off the balance you've achieved.

How you both deal with it will be individual and unique to your relationship. There's obviously no right way; there's only the way that works best for you. To the extent you plan for these changes before they happen, the better off you'll be.

Conclusion

At this stop on our roadmap, I addressed some of the changes you will face regarding your career and work. For some of you, this will be a huge transition that leaves you isolated, unsure of yourself, and uncertain of the future. That can be a stressful place, which can lead to depression or simply unhappiness. Ultimately those feelings can lead to difficulties with relationships. But, to take what I hope is a useful philosophical approach, uncertainty is also the best place to grow from. If you know where you're going (or hope to go), then you'll head in that direction. If you don't know or are uncertain, you might try different paths, some of which can lead you to greener pastures.

In the next chapter, our roadmap will take us to a discussion of ways to fill some of the space that is created by the transition away from our full-time work.

CHAPTER

What Do You Want to Do with the Rest of Your Life?

■ ■ ■

You've grown up—and then some. So now what? What's your game plan? Do you even have one? As I explained in earlier chapters, getting to a point in your life where you are easing up on job responsibilities and facing choices about how to fill leisure time can be overwhelming, exciting, and challenging. If you're at that point, this chapter is for you. If that point is years away, this chapter is for you as well; I recommend that you read it with an eye on what's ahead. Keep in mind, though, that life can bring unexpected changes. Whether you win the lottery, reduce your work hours, or retire completely, you'll eventually face the unknown of having a great deal of leisure time. In this chapter, I discuss some ways to fill that time by trying out some of these options:

- Pursuing hobbies.
- Working part-time.
- Starting a business or consulting.
- Volunteering.
- Going back to school.

- Traveling.
- Writing.
- Completing your own bucket list.

Some of us handle retirement and increased leisure time with grace; others approach it with dread. Inevitably, almost all of us will have to face the fact that our careers either have ended, are about to end, or are winding down. It may be in your 50s or much later. (As I said earlier, almost three-quarters of us think that we'll work, whether because we want to or need to, well past 65.) Ultimately, though, you'll wake up one day and not have to go to work or be responsible for something. Life will be a bunch of Saturdays strung together. How you plan now will determine to a great extent whether you create the life you want or stumble around a bit in search of it.

Nothing's wrong with stumbling around, of course, unless it creates anxiety for you or your family. If you dread the day when you don't have to go to work, if you're afraid you'll wither and die, then I encourage you to read this chapter carefully. By seeing the options you have and the processes you can take, you'll get a glimmer of what life can be for you when your job is no longer your driving force. So in this chapter, I suggest creative ways to engage in active leisure time, including a guide to completing your bucket list. Avoid value judgments (yours and others) about what you have chosen to do or not do, and don't worry about just doing nothing.

Throughout this process you will have to pay close attention to where you are on the level of activity (LOA) scale presented in Chapter 1. You'll want to be sure that your concept of leisure time is consistent with what you are realistically suited for. That's not to say you are stuck in one particular level of the scale—you can certainly move up that if you want. But you should at least know where you are now.

Similarly, if through injury, illness, loss of strength, or loss of motivation, you are no longer physically as able as you once were and find you have moved to a lower LOA level, your mental health and life satisfaction will be much influenced by accepting that change. If, for example, your vision of leisure time was to play tennis but you now find you are physically unable to run on the tennis court, you may have to adjust that goal and find an alternative. Maybe over time you'll be able to play again. But if not, first start by knowing exactly what it is about that leisure activity you enjoy. If it's the physical exertion, then you may be able to substitute another activity to fill that need. If it's the competition, or camaraderie, or something else, knowing specifically what you get out of playing tennis will help you find substitutes that provide similar rewards.

So let's start with some of the most common pursuits.

Hobbies

Chances are that somewhere along the way you had a hobby. Maybe as a kid you collected stamps. Or maybe you tried sewing or gardening. You chose that activity because it gave you pleasure and you were usually able to accomplish something. Maybe you made the world's longest afghan or managed to rid your garden of aphids while protecting the precious tomatoes. Maybe your hobby was athletic or perhaps it was something less active, like reading. The activity gave you pleasure, you found you could do it for a period of time without being bored, and you could go back to it somewhat routinely. Maybe you had a standing golf game with your buddies; maybe you became a gym rat, working out and socializing with others who enjoyed being there. Maybe you picked up the guitar or sat down at the piano and hammered out a few tunes. When you got a little more proficient, maybe you decided to take a few lessons and enjoyed them quite a bit. Or you sang in a local choir—sponsored by your school, house of worship, or local group. These activities kept you occupied and gave you a great deal of satisfaction. If they didn't, you would have stopped doing them (at least after your mother stopped insisting you practice). You persisted for at least some period of time. Maybe you stopped as you got busier or when the activity lost its appeal. Or maybe you, like I, felt you were no longer capable of playing baseball well, so you stopped rather than be the last one chosen in a pick-up game.

I'm willing to bet that a lot of you, older now and caught up in the business of life, say to yourselves, "I have no hobbies." But I'm also willing to bet that many of you *do* have hobbies—it's just that, whether you downplay their importance or give them short shrift, you don't call them by that name.

A hobby is nothing more than a leisure activity you enjoy doing on a regular basis. It can be as simple as browsing the Internet, reading blogs, or playing computer games or as formal as participating in a special club. A hobby may even earn you some money. You may know folks who regularly sell stuff at flea markets or online. There's a borderline, however, when money is involved: If you're written a novel that sits on your shelf (or in your computer's hard drive), it's a hobby. When it sells, it's a business—according to the Internal Revenue Service, anyway.

Tip

The IRS has very specific rules and definitions of whether an activity is a business or hobby and whether, as a result, expenses you incur in doing it can be considered business expenses that offset any of the financial gain. In general, an activity qualifies as a business if it is carried on with the reasonable expectation of earning a profit. The IRS presumes that an activity is carried on for profit and is, therefore, a business, if it makes a profit during at least three of the last five tax years. Here are the questions you must consider, and what the IRS will look at, to determine the distinctions:

- Does the time and effort put into the activity indicate an intention to make a profit?
- Do you depend on income from the activity?
- Are losses, if any, due to circumstances beyond your control or did they occur in the start-up phase of the business?
- Do you have the knowledge needed to carry on the activity as a successful business?
- Have you made a profit in similar activities in the past?
- Does the activity make a profit in some years?
- Can you expect to make a profit in the future from the appreciation of assets used in the activity?

So let's explore the notion of finding a hobby, particularly for those of you who claim to have none. First, let's revisit Chapter 2 and my "Ten Steps to Creating Your Life Goals" list.

The first step asks you to "observe yourself." To me, this applies perfectly to creating your hobby. The fact is you are already doing in your spare time what you like to do. Call it a hobby, call it your leisure time activity, or call it keeping busy. Maybe it's in the evening after work and dinner when you sit and watch TV. Or on a Saturday or Sunday morning when you sit with a cup of coffee and read the paper, go to the farmer's market, or work out at the gym. You have many options for how you spend your admittedly limited amount of time. The activity you choose to do in that time is called your hobby. Don't put a value judgment on whether it's a good thing or a bad thing. It's just something you do. There are probably other endeavors that would bring other rewards—some that others will *say* are more meaningful or productive. But if you like your hobby, don't deny or condemn it—just accept it. You're not stuck doing it for the rest of your life. It's what you like doing now.

For instance, you may love playing basketball with your buddies, but if you develop arthritis in your knees, you may decide to play less or coach a kids' team. You may hang out on the couch watching old movies on cold winter afternoons, but when summer comes you prefer to go swimming in the lake. Your hobbies are likely to change as you move around on the level of activity scale, as you develop new interests, when you move to a different house or town, or when your financial status changes.

Just as the first step to creating life goals is relevant to creating your hobby, so too are all the other steps in the list. You can brainstorm, visualize, and not judge yourself or your choices of hobby. You can observe others to see if what they do for pleasure appeals to you (as I say, "If you try it on and it fits, it's yours"). You can be specific, write your ideas down, share them with others, analyze them, and categorize them to help you. Ultimately these steps will lead you to accepting that you do, in fact, have a hobby, and to explore others.

The two best pieces of advice I can offer about choosing hobbies are these:

1. Accept that what it is you do in your spare time is what you like to do.
2. Don't judge what you choose.

111

Part-Time Work

Transitioning from your full-time job to retirement is a major life change that can induce anxiety. Most of the people I've spoken with about it dreaded the day when they no longer had anything productive to do. Setting aside the value judgments, you can find ways to minimize the stress, ease into the transition, and perhaps bring in some extra income at the same time by working part time. The money can help with expenses, increase your nest egg, or serve as "mad money" to be used for a special trip or purchase.

Now to be honest, part-time work is not always easy to come by. Sometimes the income is so meager that it's hardly worth the effort. But for many people, it's quite an attractive option. For a good source on the topic, read Kerry Hannon's *AARP Great Jobs for Everyone 50+: How to Find Work That Keeps You Happy and Healthy . . . and Pays the Bills* (John Wiley & Sons, 2012).

If the idea of working part time is attractive to you, I offer the following 10 suggestions:

1. Speak with your current employer or supervisor about continuing your current job on a part-time basis, such as 20 hours a week. Offer to decrease or give up benefits, if that makes your employer more amenable.
2. Speak with your current employer or supervisor about working on a specific project related to your current job that doesn't require you to work full time.
3. After clearing it with your current employer or supervisor, speak with customers, clients, or colleagues about the possibility of working part time or on a project.
4. Investigate job opportunities in your field at other companies or organizations where your experience may give you an edge. Make sure you don't have any restrictions on working for a competitor before you apply or accept a position.
5. If you volunteer or assist with an organization, speak to the appropriate people about the possibility of working there on a part-time basis. Since they know you and your work, they may offer you opportunities to take on additional responsibilities.

6. If you don't already, volunteer! Sometimes you can get into an organization, demonstrate your work, and then, as in the previous tip, move into a paid position.

7. Investigate a change of career. This will throw you into the full applicant pool with others new to the field, but your life and job experience might give you an edge, particularly if you are clear that you are looking only for part-time or short-term work.

8. If you're interested in retail work, speak with the merchants you frequent about the possibility of being hired as a salesperson.

9. NETWORK! I can't overemphasize the importance of speaking with others and making it known that you are interested in working part time. There's a great chance that at least one of the people you know or interact with is looking for someone trustworthy and diligent, traits you have likely displayed in your dealings with that person.

10. Be active in online social networking. That includes the current large ones (e.g., Facebook, Twitter, LinkedIn, Elance, or PeoplePerHour) and others that are either new or specific to a field. You can post your résumé and apply for projects and jobs through many of these outlets. Online networks will increase your visibility enormously. But be wary of privacy concerns and scams.

Starting a Business or Consulting

If you've always dreamed about being your own boss, maybe now's your time! Starting a business—large or small—can be the most rewarding experience in your life. It can also be the toughest, most frustrating, and least profitable way to make a buck.

But if you know all of that going in, you're ahead of the game. And if you have realistic expectations—including the notion that you may barely break even—making the transition from full-time employee to business owner can be a joy.

Myriad books and articles on the Internet describe the best ways and most successful business start-ups, including franchising. I don't attempt here to summarize or expand on those; the topic is beyond the scope of this book. Instead, I raise some issues to consider if starting a business or consulting seems like an appealing option as you switch gears in (or leave) the career track.

You should know a few factors about starting a business, particularly as it affects your tax liability. As I mentioned in the section on hobbies, business expenses are legitimate write-offs for your taxes. Those write-offs can include all the actual out-of-pocket expenses you have, such as marketing, travel, legal expenses, and supplies, as well as the cost of having your office in your home. Under specific rules, you can deduct from your income certain easily tracked home-office expenses such as portions of your mortgage or rent, utilities, insurance, and maintenance. But, as I also explained in the section on hobbies, you must meet specific criteria for your leisure-time activity to be considered a business by the IRS. The most important thing regarding a business is not that you actually *make* a profit, but that you clearly intend to make a profit. So if you have a business loss for a few years, that's acceptable.

Although there's no hard and fast rule about how many years you can carry on your business without making a profit, a business that makes a profit in three of the last five years would definitely qualify. But don't be dissuaded from claiming that you are starting a business because you don't have a profit. Many legitimate businesses take quite a long time before the bottom line changes from red to black. If you have any question about whether or not to claim your activity is a business or a hobby, consult with your tax adviser.

Tip

You may have to report income you receive, regardless of whether it is from an activity considered to be a business or a hobby. Be sure to check with a tax adviser.

I emphasize once more that this section is not about how to start a business, but rather, how to spend your leisure time. Consider yourself successfully employed (that is, occupied) if you start an enterprise that you enjoy and keeps you active and involved. As long as you don't need the money, any income you receive will be a plus that you may or may not be able to offset with business expenses.

Tip

Most business owners will tell you that working for themselves and starting a business is the hardest work they've ever done. If your vision of having a business entails sleeping in, working a handful of hours a day, and chillin' on the beach the rest of the time, you may be in for a rude awakening. You can run certain businesses, such as being a consultant, in limited hours. If you are looking at this option to keep busy and productive, you should do a great deal of research about the business you are considering so you jump in with realistic expectations.

Volunteering

If you've always thought, "There are so many things I can do to help, and I've always wanted to help [insert your cause here]," you're right. There are many causes to believe in and organizations to support—and so many of those need your help. What's more, serving as a volunteer will provide you with enormous personal rewards *and* allow you to be challenged and engaged. In fact, when you first start thinking about the volunteering options you'll have with more spare time, the more likely you'll be overwhelmed. Ironically, though, it seems as if the people who've been volunteering already start doing so even more frequently and for more hours. It's like that unofficial rule: If you want to get something done, ask the busiest person to do it! That Type A executive who jogs daily also likely serves on nonprofit boards or helps in a soup kitchen.

If you've already been active with volunteer organizations, civic activities, religious groups, or any other kind of unpaid work, chances are there are many more things and many more related organizations that can use both your help and your extra free time.

To help you get started volunteering, review the steps above about finding a hobby. Choosing the right place to volunteer will likely be similar to choosing your hobby. First, observe yourself. What you now do in your spare time—and the organizations you support—are those same ones you might want to volunteer for. On the other hand, if you're already doing some work for an organization, you might decide that with more spare time you now want to branch out into other areas. Observing what you do now doesn't limit you. It only gives you a clear snapshot of yourself and the places where you've been devoting your energy. Once you see the picture, you're free to change it all you want.

Tip

When you think about the organization you want to volunteer for, consider where you are on the level of activity scale. There are many roles to fill and tasks to be done in these organizations. Be sure to pin down what your job description entails so you can be sure you can physically handle the work. If you have difficulty standing for long periods or cannot lift heavy packages, for instance, you'll want to be sure you don't set yourself up for an unrewarding and unsatisfying experience by volunteering in a busy mailroom. And you don't want the organization to think you are lazy or regard your work as unsatisfactory. So when you are discussing volunteer work, be sure to get as specific as you can about the actual work you'll be doing.

But volunteer work can differ significantly from a hobby. First, it may offer opportunities unique from any you've had before. For example, if you've always wanted to travel to Africa, volunteering for one of the great organizations that assists in small villages might offer the chance to combine your altruistic tendencies with your desire to explore. If you've been interested in politics, you may decide to get involved with a campaign, something you never had time for—and couldn't do if you worked in the public sector.

Volunteer work also differs from hobbies in terms of the outside commitment you make. When you agree to work for an organization, it becomes more than just something you do to keep busy and challenged. The organization you work for will come to rely on you, perhaps sometimes heavily. Most places have a very limited paid staff and tend to depend on volunteers to do the lion's share of the work. So I encourage you at the start to inform the staff about the amount of time you can devote. That's not to say that you can't reduce your hours or change jobs within the organization, but the longer you are there, the more difficult it may be to pull back.

There are many resources for finding the appropriate volunteer opportunity for you beyond where you currently work or volunteer. If you're looking to expand your horizons, you can do an easy search by location at www.createthegood.org, www.volunteermatch .org, and www.serve.gov. There is no shortage of possibilities, with more than 25,000 hits resulting from an Internet search for volunteer matching services.

Life Story

Paul had been a college administrator for many years; his wife, Jean, was a nurse. When they retired, they both had a strong desire to volunteer for some worthy cause and, in particular, they wanted to go back to Africa, where they had visited years before. They knew there were many wonderful opportunities but didn't know what they involved or for whom. They searched the Internet for "Africa volunteer," and up popped about 50 million hits. They browsed through the first few pages and eliminated all the organizations whose cause didn't meet their standards or beliefs. And they quickly eliminated all of the organizations that required them to pay to apply; although they understood the need to charge—some volunteer organizations get inundated with applications and need staff to review them—the couple didn't want to pay much up front. They were also interested in small start-ups, because Paul liked the idea of being a part of building something from the ground up. They chose an organization that fit their needs and have since visited Africa many times. Initially, Paul was concerned that while Jean had a specific expertise, he didn't. It turned out, though, that his skills at organizing and recruiting other volunteers proved valuable. And just as important as the satisfaction and good feelings they have gotten from helping people in a small village in Uganda, they've made great friendships, a reward neither of them anticipated.

Back to School

For many of us, school was a necessity, not something we looked forward to. But as I got a little older, I saw education in a totally different light. I started to value learning as an opportunity, not an obligation. As you start to think about your leisure time, you might want to consider going back to school as an option. What's particularly important now, compared to a mere decade ago, is the proliferation of online courses, which makes physical limitations and geography no longer a barrier. Following are the various types of school programs you might consider.

- *Osher Lifelong Learning Institutes (OLLI):* Under the sponsorship of the Bernard Osher Foundation, the Osher Lifelong Learning Institutes offer programs at more than 100 colleges and universities. These noncredit courses are designed for people 50 and older who are interested in taking courses for personal enrichment and the joy of learning. Costs vary, but typically membership includes access to college facilities and one or two courses, covering a wide range of topics, per semester. Find more information at www .osherfoundation.org.
- *Local colleges:* Many college and universities offer the opportunity to audit classes for no cost, although you may have to pay for books and supplies. Most colleges have some options available, but each individual department may have its own rules, requirements, and space constraints (due to overcrowding). The best news is that you get to participate in the class but don't have to take the tests!
- *Continuing education:* Colleges and universities, as well as local recreation centers, YMCAs, and other similar associations in most communities, offer classes for people interested in a wide range of topics. The courses are inexpensive and well attended.
- *Certificate programs:* If you are interested in a new area of study or a new line of work, you can enroll in a certificate program at a college (especially a community college where the costs are much lower) in a variety of areas such as project management

or human resources management. Such programs may help you find part-time or consulting positions.

- *Seminars and workshops:* Colleges and universities often offer noncredit seminars and workshops open to the public and in a variety of subjects. The fees are usually quite low.
- *Courses to maintain credentials:* If you are interested in maintaining your current credential, local colleges and universities may offer the required courses for a modest fee. This can help you if you decide to work part time or consult.
- *Graduate or undergraduate programs:* If you're considering changing careers or advancing in your career, this may be a great time to enroll in a degree program. A great many resources are available, and you can investigate getting low-interest federally guaranteed student loans and scholarships from a variety of sources. If you're going to finally get that bachelor's degree you always wanted, you may even qualify for other need-based aid, depending on your income. You can get information about paying for college at www .collegeboard.org.
- *MOOCs (Massive Open Online Courses):* Many of the leading colleges and universities have developed online courses that are available to anyone around the globe, usually for no cost (or with a minimal cost if you want to earn college credit). A huge portfolio of online courses allows you to learn at your own pace and on your own time. You have the opportunity to telecommute to campus from anywhere—including the comfort of your office or home. Furthermore, you are not restricted to a local college. You can enroll in both credit and noncredit courses at leading universities across the country or, in fact, throughout the world. The list is endless, and a quick Internet search will yield literally millions of possibilities, some leading to degrees, some just for knowledge. Perhaps your own alma mater or local campus offers online courses that you can take. You can find an MOOC through aggregators, where you can explore many options (such as www.class-central.com or www.mooc-list .com), but since this is a growing area, the best way to find what you'd like is to search the Internet for MOOC.

Travel

Just about everyone I've spoken with about how they intend to spend their later years mentions travel. It's a pastime that so many people love and that creates lasting memories. Meeting people from other parts of the world—or even other parts of the country—can be so rewarding on so many levels. I love to travel and have visited all but one continent, each several times, and every U.S. state.

At the same time, there are many aspects of travel that are not quite so positive. It's important that you recognize the difficulties, barriers, and stresses that may accompany you on a trip. But let me talk about some of the opportunities before I get into the concerns.

Travel Opportunities

Following is a list of some ways people have arranged various trips.

- *Tours:* Most everyone is aware of the many tour companies that put together trips to just about everywhere. An organized tour can be a great way to learn about a place and is most appropriate for people who aren't experienced travelers or who like to have the travel and itineraries worked out for them. It's also a great way for singles to travel, since you can meet interesting people on such trips. Working with a respected travel agent is a good way to learn about various tours, and generally it doesn't cost you any more than if you book a tour yourself. In fact, it may cost you less because a good agent works with many tour operators and can often get a better deal than an individual. Finding the right tour company can be a challenge, not only because so many exist but because of the potential to get ripped off. AARP is a great resource (www.aarp.org/travel).

- *University-sponsored trips:* Often college alumni groups sponsor tours, although not all the travelers who sign up are alums. Advertising through an alumni group may be a way to attract individuals who are inclined to attend the lectures and other educational opportunities offered in addition to touring, or to extend word-of-mouth invitations to alums from other universities or to friends of alums.

- *Road Scholar:* Previously called Elderhostel, Road Scholar offers various educational travel opportunities to people who are 55 and older. Road Scholar is a not-for-profit organization whose educational trips include cultural outings, discussions, and meetings all over the world. The company provides experts who lead discussions and inform participants about the areas they are exploring. This type of tour is particularly good for singles who want to travel with others sharing similar interests. You can learn more by visiting www .roadscholar.org.

- *Frequent flyer miles and frequent guest points:* For those who have frequent flyer miles or frequent guest points at hotels, this is a fantastic way to travel and reduce expenses enormously. I confess that my wife and I have accumulated many, many miles and points and have used this method many times. There are certainly barriers to getting flights (though fewer barriers with hotels), but booking far in advance can better your chances. You can generally book reward travel 331 days in advance, so it's important to plan and book early to take advantage of these free tickets. If you're trying to fly first class or business class, the airline may release only one seat at a time. That can be frustrating, but if you can work with the airline, you can generally get the second seat later on when the inventory is released. (You are usually put in economy class and waitlisted for first class.) The key, as I said, is early planning. You'll also be more successful if you can be very flexible on dates.

- *Expeditions:* Whether you're traveling solo or not, this kind of travel has become very popular because many adventurous people seek out experiences that are unique. You can go on that safari you've always wanted; explore exotic places like Borneo and the mountains of Thailand, staying with hill tribe people; cruise the Amazon River; visit Antarctica or the Galapagos Islands; and so forth. Some of the trips are a bit more rugged, some less so. You are usually better off with guides or an organized tour company. Some trips are specifically designed for people with limited mobility. Most travel agencies in your area can hook you up with excellent expedition tour companies, including some famous ones such as www.nationalgeographicexpeditions.com and www .linbladexpeditions.com. Often these expedition companies specialize in specific regions of the world.

- *Cruising:* There are cruise people and there are non-cruise people. There are many types of cruises—big or small, adventurous and relaxing, family-oriented or romantic—to accommodate all but those adamantly opposed to traveling by ship. One of the great things about cruising is that it is a terrific opportunity for people with limited mobility to experience new things. It's also great for singles, since there are others on board with whom to interact, and for people traveling with families. Internet searches will yield millions of results, and here, too, I suggest that you work with a travel agent. The agent can help you find the best itinerary and ship as well as the best deals.

- *Volunteer vacations:* Many organizations sponsor trips on which you volunteer your time and expertise to local projects in the United States and abroad, participating in so-called voluntourism. Read the Life Story about my friends Paul and Jean, who volunteered for an organization that worked in Africa. Many opportunities are available and you can use the AARP search referred to above (www.createthegood.org) on which organizations post opportunities. You can also search the Internet for volunteer vacations and find millions of possibilities. Like with MOOCs, there are aggregators of these opportunities such as www.volunteerguide.org, www .globeaware.org, and www.globalvolunteers.org.

- *RVing:* A popular type of travel opportunity involves loading up your basic household goods—and your pets—into a van of just about any size and heading out on the highways and byways. You can explore at your own pace, and there are thousands of places to hook up to electricity, water, and sewer. The recreational vehicles themselves can be bought or rented and are quite expensive—as is the gas you will use, because the gas mileage is so low. But you'll save on hotel and other transportation costs, plus you'll be able to bring along your beloved pets. Many websites and books are devoted to RVing. If you're planning to take an RV on the road, be sure you like to drive or be in a vehicle for long periods, since that's essentially what you'll be doing. You also won't be able to park or hook up to facilities in most cities, so you'll need to figure out transportation to and from the sites you want to visit.

Travel Concerns

While travel can be exciting, fascinating, relaxing, and otherwise a totally enjoyable experience, it can also be frustrating, challenging, and fraught with major concerns, not the least of which is danger. Certainly there are parts of the world that are a bit more risky to visit than Disney World. If you are planning to visit any one of those more exotic destinations, check the U.S. Department of State to access the latest information. At www.state.gov, you can find travel alerts as well as important information about specific places (such as whether you need a visa and the location of the U.S. Embassy).

Even if you've researched all the crucial details, other aspects of exotic travel can ruin an otherwise fantastic trip. Personal health and safety are always primary concerns, but I believe that taking appropriate precautions is about all you can do to minimize risk. You can get run over by the proverbial bus anywhere (including at Disney World); you can get sick anywhere. Take heed, be conscious of your surroundings, plan your trip well, and learn as much as you can about the places you are visiting. Always have a Plan B for when things go awry, whether that includes carrying a cell phone for emergencies (one that works in the place you are visiting) or packing extra medications. To prepare, here are some concerns you should consider.

- *LOA:* Where you are on the level of activity scale should play an important role in planning your trip. If, for example, your expedition is meant for people who are very active, you should find out just how active that means, particularly if you have any mobility limitations. Opportunities to travel and experience the richness of our world are available to anyone, regardless of their physical abilities, if you do your research and choose accordingly. At the same time, don't assume your LOA needs to limit you. If you're not able to ski, you may still want to go to Park City, Utah, during the winter for all the other opportunities available, such as the Sundance Film Festival every January.

- *Expenses:* You can travel on the cheap or in luxury. It's up to you. And you'll have a great time either way as long as you are comfortable with the amount you are spending. If you budget $5,000 and realize that you have severely under-budgeted, you will not enjoy your experience. Similarly, if you are within your budget but realize the accommodations are not up to your standards or expectations, you will be unhappy and the experience will not be pleasant. Do as much research as you can so you know what to expect and to determine whether the kind of trip fits into the lifestyle you want and most enjoy.

- *Availability of hotels and flights:* To me, there's nothing worse than traveling to a city and not knowing whether I have a place to sleep that night. That uncertainty haunts me all day, so to alleviate that concern my wife and I either preplan or find a place first thing in the morning. Other folks may be comfortable winging it. Knowing what you like (and what gets to you) is the first step in planning for a great travel experience. Another consideration regarding availability is maximizing your chances to cash in frequent flyer miles and hotel guest points. It can be so frustrating to have thousands and thousands of miles but not be able to use them. I discuss this above but want to repeat here that when it comes to frequent flyer miles, the key is to plan early! You're generally allowed to book flights 331 days in advance. If you do that, you'll have a much greater chance of using your miles and points before they expire.

- *Pets:* Unless you are driving or are willing to pay the extra money to fly your pet, you'll have to make arrangements for any pets you leave at home. For me, with two dogs, this is a major deal. Early planning is the best way to ensure that you have your pets covered. Options include kennels, boarding places, and local "nannies" who will take your pet in or housesit while you're away. More and more hotels and motels allow pets these days, usually for an additional fee, but most of these places limit the number of rooms where pets can stay, so make your plans early to ensure availability.

- *Delays:* Delays occur for all kinds of reasons, including weather and mechanical troubles. Some are unavoidable, or at least beyond your control. But you can minimize the likelihood of others, and more important, lessen their impact. If you're heading to an island paradise served by just one flight per day, you sure don't want to miss your connection because of something you can prevent, such as allowing insufficient time between connecting flights, not accounting for traffic on the way to the airport, or underestimating the time it takes to get through a security check. The extra time you spend at the airport is worth reducing the risk of missing a key flight. To minimize the risk of delays, try to avoid driving to the airport or flying during rush hour. In the summer you probably want to avoid late afternoon flights because of thunderstorms (although they also happen in the mornings, too). Pay attention to the weather reports in your departure, connecting, and arrival cities. If you're driving to your destination, map out the route and try to avoid traveling in high-traffic areas during rush hour. Sometimes an alternate route may wind up being faster, even though it is longer in mileage. Many websites and online tools can help you with these kinds of travel tips.

- *Singles:* Many tours, cruises, and prepaid trips base their rates on double occupancy and charge a "single supplement," which can be quite significant—as much as 50 percent more than half of the double rate. To use a simple example, if the double occupancy rate is $100, the single rate could be as much as $75 (i.e., 50 percent more than $50). Plan accordingly. If you have a friend with whom you're comfortable traveling, that's one way for both of you to save money. But if it means you're miserable sharing the cramped quarters and it ruins your trip, it was probably not a great way to cut costs. You can explore this area more in AARP's

The Single Woman's Guide to Retirement (John Wiley & Sons, 2012), by Jan Cullinane.

Writing (Your Memoirs?)

Leisure time is a great time to write, whether you're going to write the Great American Novel, letters (to friends and relatives certainly, but also to newspaper and magazine editors), or blogs. If you've always had a hankering, then maybe now's the time.

One of the best ways to start—let's face it, a blank page or screen can be intimidating—is to write about your life. After all, every one of us has a story! And most of the time it's quite interesting, not just to ourselves but to our kids and grandkids, too. It's our way of preserving history and helping future generations find their roots. In the discussion of family and relationships in Chapter 11, I talk about composing that all-important letter to your loved ones and perhaps putting together an ethical will. But here I want to encourage you to write your life story.

Sit down at your computer and start from the beginning. Don't edit yourself and don't limit yourself—at least not when you first start. Just start typing and see where it goes. You'll be amazed at how easily things start rolling. Be sure to include as many anecdotes as you can remember, since that will add all the color and personality to your story. Explain to your reader all about your family history, where you grew up, what it was like for you. Pretend your young grandchild is sitting on your lap, enraptured by your stories of how it was when you were young. What was going on in the world when you were your grandchild's age?

I recommend focusing in particular on what was happening in the world—and your personal world—when you were about 14 until about 17 or 18. There's a theory that what you are now is what you were at the age when you started to form your philosophy of life, your awareness of who you were. That generally happens to people in their mid-teens. So explain to your reader what was significant to you then. Talk about the feelings you had.

Then go on to talk about your later years, your career, and your current family. It's a fun exercise and I can assure you that you'll enjoy it. Don't worry about getting the perfect words or even about spelling or grammar. Get the stories out. Your family will love having it.

If writing becomes your hobby, that's great. Keep going and maybe you really will write the Great American Novel. But most important is providing history, your history, for future generations.

Life Story

My father was born into a working-class family in 1913. His parents and most of his relatives had emigrated from Eastern Europe and, like most immigrants, struggled to make a living in the United States. During the Great Depression in the 1920s, he left school to work in whatever job he could find to help the family put food on the table. The Depression had a lasting impression on him—as it did on most people who lived through those tough years. He learned that he couldn't rely on tomorrow and that education brought more opportunity. He also learned to not trust credit. He needed to own things outright. For the remainder of his life, he rarely borrowed money, forgoing credit cards and home loans.

He later earned his college degree and became a lawyer. He insisted that all of his children go to college, and he focused his law practice on helping those people who didn't have the kind of opportunity he was able to provide for us.

Many years later, when he finally agreed to write about his life—prodded, I confess, by his kids—he didn't want to say much about his early years, choosing instead to write about better times, both before and after those tough years. My father never got to finish his memoir, but the pages he did write are cherished gifts to my family.

Completing Your Bucket List

Much has been written about creating and completing a "bucket list," that is, a list of accomplishments you want to achieve or experiences you'd like to have during your life. It's a great catchphrase and captures well the notion that our lives are limited, so let's live them to the fullest if we can. The following 10 tips on completing your bucket list are drawn from the experience of creating my own.

Ten Tips for Creating and Completing Your Bucket List

1. *Observe yourself.* When thinking about the items you'd like to put on your bucket list, draw on what you observe in your own behavior, just as you did when creating your list of goals and hobbies. Taking note of your likes and dislikes—the things that motivate you to act (or not)—can help you create and, ultimately, complete the list.

2. *Extend what you do.* Once you know what you like to do, it's not a large jump to creating a new item for your list. If you've really enjoyed fishing, for example, you can take that to a new height for your bucket list by, say, enrolling in a fishing school or entering a fishing rodeo. If you love watching TV, you might want to make your own TV show or help out at a local station. During a pledge drive for a small non-profit station, I got to run a camera and host the drive for a half hour.

3. *Observe others.* Looking at what others do or have on their bucket lists is a great way to realize your own aspirations. "Hey, look at what he's doing, or what's on her list. That looks cool!"

4. *Daydream.* Let your imagination run wild.

5. *Be realistic.* Take that wild imagination and try to rein it in a bit. You might dream of taking a trip into space, but unless you have a whole lot of money or know someone who owns a spaceship, there's not a great chance you'll complete this item. Your level of activity scale will also limit your bucket list.

6. *Be specific.* A bucket list cannot be vague or general; otherwise it falls more into the category of a goal. The more specific you are, the easier it will be to complete the list. But equally important, the more specific you are, the easier it will be to create the list in the first place, since multiple items can emerge from one type of activity. "Learn Spanish" may be too vague. Instead, try "Learn Spanish well enough to have a conversation with a native speaker, without using English." Then you can also include "take a trip to Mexico" as another bucket list item.

7. *Revisit your list periodically.* The list is not static. You should check it periodically to see if what's on the list should still be there and remains a possibility. Ten years from now you may not want to bungee jump off a bridge.

8. *Think about the process of creating your list.* What does the list tell you about yourself? Who are you? What does having a bucket list mean to you?

9. *Think about what it actually takes to complete an item.* Accomplishing or completing an item may be its own reward. But in analyzing what's involved, you might discover that the process is not attractive to you. If one of your bucket list items is to take a road trip across the country and back, remember that you'd likely be spending 90 hours or more actually driving (equivalent to roughly eight 12-hour days of driving). If you get seasick, you need to know that skydiving also means hanging from a parachute for about six minutes, during which time many people experience mild to strong nausea.

10. *Learn from other items on your bucket list.* When you've actually accomplished an item, what did you learn from that? Was it all about the accomplishment or was it the activity itself? Was learning to play the piano all that you had hoped? If so, maybe there's something you can add to the list, such as performing in a piano recital. Or if snorkeling in the Caribbean was spectacular for you, think about learning to SCUBA dive.

Conclusion

When we were young, we were often asked, "What do you want to be when you grow up?" As I said at the beginning of this chapter, you're grown up now, and you probably don't think much about what you want to be. But my guess is, as you envision your life, especially if you're no longer employed full time, you are probably quite concerned with answering the question, "What do I want to do with the rest of my life?"

In this chapter, I hope I helped guide you toward your answer. Whether it's continuing to work, starting a business, or involving yourself in leisure and volunteer opportunities, I gave you ways to help you focus on what options are best for you. I hope I also inspired you to try new things, to explore and expand your horizons through travel or pursuing hobbies. And finally, I gave you my tips of how to create and complete your bucket list. For the record, my personal bucket list continues to shrink and grow as I accomplish some things and change my interests. I've recently added going to Antarctica to my list. And although playing shortstop is not very likely, I still haven't crossed it off.

In the next chapter we'll come back to earth to deal with some of the realities we face with transitioning to your heirs what we've accumulated in our lives thus far.

CHAPTER

Transitioning What You Own

■ ■ ■

How many times did you hear your parents say, "I don't want to be a burden to my children?"

None of us wants to be a burden on the next generation. But a host of legal problems pops up if you don't take the appropriate steps to plan for your old age. In addition, unless you take specific legal steps, you can't be sure that your estate—that is, everything you own—will go to your survivors just as you want. This chapter will help you understand the basic legal issues involved.

In this chapter, I explain the different ways you and your partner can own property—real estate, investments, or any asset—to best protect it. I discuss the three goals for lifetime planning and provide steps to ensure that in the event of a catastrophic illness, your wishes are carried out. Most of these topics fall under the umbrella of elder law, but don't be put off by the term. And don't think that you must see an elder law attorney. Most attorneys are familiar with the main areas covered here. On the other hand, if your personal, legal, and financial situation becomes more complicated, you would be wise to consult an elder law expert.

Failure to plan well for your later years financially and legally—and most people don't plan adequately—can lead to problems for you and your children in the following areas:

- Management of your own affairs.
- Life and death decisions.
- Long-term care.
- Preservation of inheritances.

As more and more of us get older, these issues will become a greater problem for society as a whole, leading to major decisions being made *for* us, not *by* us.

A Note about Notary Publics

Before diving into the specifics, I should mention that many documents you will have to sign must be notarized by a third party who testifies that the signer is the person he or she claims to be. So you will need proof of identity and must sign the document in front of the notary.

You'll probably find a notary public at your bank, brokerage, real estate office, or attorney's office. Some notaries charge a small fee, others don't. Most attorneys have a notary available in their office, so if you are having your attorney draw up a legal document, you can likely have it notarized at the same time.

Probate

One term important to mention here is probate, the process by which:

- Property is inventoried and accounted for after the person dies.
- Any debts are paid off.
- Any taxes owed are paid off.
- Whatever is left of the estate is given to the rightful heirs.

The probate process can be cumbersome and costly. Numerous fees will have to be paid: court fees, fees to file legal papers, and fees to appraisers and to other professionals. If an attorney probates the will, you'll also have to pay the attorney's fee, which can be substantial. The amount an attorney charges will vary based on the size of the estate and whether the attorney charges a flat fee or an hourly rate. For an estate valued at $100,000, the attorney's fee for probating the will generally will range from about $2,000 to $3,000.

The question, then, is, can you take steps to avoid probate? The short answer is "yes." There are a couple of ways: with certain types of joint ownership and with revocable living trusts, both of which I cover in this chapter.

Tip

Banks where you have an account, or your broker, often have notaries available and will probably not charge you to notarize a document. But they will probably not notarize anything *unless* you have an account with their firm. I have also found that some of the larger hotels have notaries available and provide the service even if you're not staying there.

Joint Ownership

The fact that you and your partner own something together, whether it's assets, real estate, or other property, does not guarantee a smooth transition when either of you dies. So it's important to understand some of the legal ins and outs regarding the four kinds of joint ownership. The type you and your partner establish will depend on your financial situation and where you live.

- **Joint tenancy**. Ownership through joint tenancy means that each of you has an undivided interest in the entire property. If one owner dies, the survivor or survivors own the property. If the property produces income, each party reports the income from his or her portion. Most ownership is joint tenancy unless otherwise stated.
- **Tenancy in common**. With tenancy in common, each person owns a portion of the property. Upon the death of a partner, that portion goes to his or her estate, not to the surviving

co-owners. There are tax advantages for some people who have property owned in this manner. For instance, if a surviving spouse is adequately provided for, a parent may want to leave a retirement account directly to a child or grandchild instead of the spouse, thereby eliminating probate.

- **Tenancy by the entirety**. This form of ownership applies only to legally married couples and in some states applies only to real estate. Each spouse has an undivided interest in the entire property, but a creditor of one spouse may not attach or sell the other spouse's portion. Neither spouse may dispose of his or her portion unless the other spouse agrees, and when one spouse dies the surviving spouse gets full ownership.
- **Community property**. In states that have enacted community property laws, each spouse is deemed to own one-half of the property acquired by the other spouse after the marriage took place or after the couple moved into the state. Check to see if you live in a community property state.

With both joint tenancy and community property, you get to avoid probate (thus saving some money and a great deal of hassle). In addition, your survivor has immediate use of the property or funds, which can be crucial when the survivor is trying to take care of obligations. But joint tenancy and community property also have two notable downsides:

1. *Unintended distributions:* Any one of the owners can remove any or all of the assets whenever he or she wants and for any purpose, with no limits. The other co-owners have no way to prevent this. Upon the death of any one of the co-owners, the money is divided among the other co-owners on a per capita basis, without regard to how much the surviving co-owners contributed.
2. *Creditor liability:* All funds are considered available to any of the co-owners. That means that any judgment against any one of the co-owners is a judgment against the asset, regardless of who contributed to the asset or account.

Three Goals of Lifetime Planning

There are three goals of estate or lifetime planning:

1. Ensuring an orderly distribution of your assets after your death, with as little taxation as possible.
2. Ensuring that you have a personal and financial management system in case you are incapacitated and unable to manage your own affairs.
3. Ensuring that if you are unable to manage your own affairs, those responsible have access to your resources and you have access to adequate health care without depleting all your resources.

In the rest of this chapter, I explain each goal in depth.

Goal #1: Ensuring an Orderly Distribution of Assets

The first goal, an orderly distribution of assets after death, can be easily accomplished through a written will or trust.

Last Wills and Testaments   A last will and testament is a critical document that transfers assets to heirs. Essentially, everyone should have a written will, regardless of age. A will, however, does more than just designate who gets your wealth after you die; indeed, there's usually little question of who gets the house or the cash. The small, less valuable personal items with high sentimental value, and the uncertainty of who gets what, usually cause the most problems in families. A written will can ensure the *orderly* distribution of these items. There are particular concerns when dealing with minor children and with same-sex partnerships and marriages. A will is particularly important for people with young children and same-sex partners, especially in states that do not recognize same-sex marriages.

A will is also essential for blended families, that is, families where the husband and wife have divorced and one or both have remarried. In such situations, a legal will is the only way to ensure that what you want done with your estate gets done. And even if your estate is meager, you still will want to ensure that your wishes are upheld. The last thing anyone wants is for the courts to have to step in to settle a family dispute. Usually no one wins in those cases except the attorneys.

When there are minor children still in the household, there's a great potential for a serious dispute about custody. This can be especially contentious with blended families and same-sex couples, even in states that recognize same-sex marriage. As a responsible parent, you owe it to your children to provide for their care by clearly listing the people you want to take the kids if you die prematurely. That individual or couple—and you should specify which half of the couple would get primary custody in case the couple break up—should agree in advance.

If you have very valuable items, you may want to bring in a professional appraiser before drawing up the will. To find an appraiser, you can check with the Appraisers Association of America, at 212-889-5404, www.appraisersassoc.org, or the American Society of Appraisers at 800-ASA-VALU or 703-478-2228, www.appraisers.org.

Many people who execute a legal will neglect to update it when a situation changes or your wishes change; don't let that be the case with you. Wills can be updated with an amendment called a codicil. If an attorney drew up the will, it's easiest (and probably cheapest) to have that same attorney make the changes. If you have a different attorney execute a new will or make changes, you should notify the first attorney in writing that you have a new will and that the old one is no longer valid.

In a will, you name one or more beneficiaries who are to receive some of your assets and property. You also name a particular person who will serve as the executor, whose role is to make sure that the property goes to the right person and that all bills are paid. That executor can be a close friend or relative. It does not have to be the attorney who drew up your will.

To be valid, a will must be written, signed, dated, and witnessed, usually by two people present when the will is signed. Recorded audio and video wills have been accepted when there are no controversies, but to be safe you should have a written, notarized will.

The key here is to make sure your wishes about your estate are met. The more detailed your will, the more likely your wishes about who gets what will be met. You don't want your survivors to go through a legal battle with relatives and friends who each say they were told "such-and-such" was to be theirs, or who simply feel because of the closeness, they "deserve" a particular item.

The cost for an attorney to draft a will likely runs from a low of about $100 up to about $1,000 or $1,500, depending on the complexity and the size of the estate. You can certainly draw up your own will, either on your own or using a software program or a pre-printed form available in many bookstores and office supply stores. If you choose any of these, however, take caution to make sure that the will is valid in your state. It would be a shame to go through the expense and trouble of drawing up the will only to have it successfully challenged because of your state laws.

Revocable Living Trusts A revocable living trust is very much like a will. It's a written document, legally prepared and witnessed; it allows you to pass on to heirs a portion of your estate after you die; and it appoints an executor or trustee, to make sure that everything is taken care of and that the terms of the trust are carried out. One major difference is that any property placed in a revocable living trust does *not* go through probate after the grantor dies.

Tip

Too many wills and trusts do not make arrangements for dearly beloved pets. If you have one, consider finding someone willing to take care of him or her, should you die (much as you would do with a minor child). You might also consider designating some money to go along with the pet to cover expenses.

Revocable living trusts have other advantages, too. You can put an age limit on when the heir gets the property, which means you don't have to worry about bequeathing property to a minor. If you become incapacitated, the trustee can handle your legal and financial affairs, thus making guardianship or conservatorship (which I talk about below) unnecessary. If you own property in more than one state, it is a good idea to put the out-of-state property in a trust so it does not have to go through probate in more than one state. And a trust is totally private in most states while a will is a public document, open to anyone once it is submitted for probate.

The primary disadvantages of a living trust are that drawing one up is more expensive—about twice at much—as a will. Attorneys and companies that set up trusts often require a minimum value. For many people, a trust is unnecessary. If your estate is relatively small, the executor of your will can handle probate with no cost and a minimum of hassle, especially if your state offers assistance to "do-it-yourself" probate or an expedited probate.

For more information about revocable living trusts, consult an attorney or financial adviser.

Tip

Some airlines, hotels, and reward programs allow you to leave to your survivors your frequent flyer miles, hotel guest points, and other reward points. Some require very specific wording, proof of death, and inclusion in your will. Those points and miles do not automatically become a part of your estate. If you have a significant number of miles or points in a program, you should investigate that program and make sure you deal with the requirements in your will.

Goal #2: Making Sure Your Affairs Are Managed

The second goal of estate or lifetime planning is ensuring that there is a system in place if you become unable to manage your own affairs. This goal is also relatively simple to accomplish. It requires only that you complete certain legal documents under the direction of a professional. Each of these has a specific purpose:

- Power of attorney.
- Durable power of attorney.
- Living wills (also called health care instructions or advance directives).
- Health-care proxy (also called health-care directive or health-care power of attorney).

Power of Attorney Simply put, a power of attorney is a legal document that authorizes another person to act as your agent or as your attorney. It is a simple document that many feel can be executed without an attorney, although you will need to have your signature notarized. But because of the potential ramifications (you are giving over a great deal of responsibility and authority to another person), you should give serious thought to who you appoint, particularly if your estate is significant.

Signing over the power to act as your attorney or agent is a serious matter and I do not recommend you enter into this lightly. You should be aware that by signing a power of attorney, you are giving the person you select the power to conduct your business. If specified in the document, that would include such things as selling and buying stocks, bonds, or property; obtaining insurance; and signing contracts on your behalf.

A power of attorney essentially gives the person designated the power to manage funds, sign contracts, and transact most business on your behalf while you are still alive and capable of making those decisions yourself. It is the kind of paper you might have if you travel a great deal or spend the winters in a warm climate but the summers elsewhere. The power can be as limited as you wish (as long as it is spelled out clearly) and can be terminated at any time by revoking the power *in writing.* Powers of attorney must be signed, dated, and notarized.

The power of attorney should also include the ability to engage in estate planning. Some states require the power of attorney document to specifically include gifting authority as well as the authority to create revocable and irrevocable trusts and to change or modify ownership interests and beneficiary designations for life insurance and annuities and retirement savings accounts, all of which are often essential to an estate plan. You should contact an attorney to determine whether in your state the general power to "conduct all business" includes the ability to make gifts on your behalf or engage in estate or planning.

A durable power of attorney is an essential tool in estate planning, particularly if you become incapacitated. A power of attorney can be limited to specific areas of responsibility (such as signing a contract for a house sale) or give broader powers to simply act on your behalf.

But it's also extremely important that the power of attorney be as specific as possible. For example, you can set up a *springing power of attorney* that goes in effect only if the signer is declared incapable.

A power of attorney does *not* mean you give up decision-making authority. Rather, it is an extremely useful tool you can use to handle your business affairs.

Note

If you become incapacited through dementia, Alzheimer's, or serious illness or accident, a regular power of attorney is automatically terminated. Under those circumstances, the person you've designated would no longer have the legal authority to conduct your business. In that case, you'll need a durable power of attorney to appoint someone to act for you.

Durable Power of Attorney   A durable power of attorney is a special kind of document that allows someone to act on your behalf *even if you become incapacitated.* This fact must be stated in the document itself by including words such as these:

I hereby make, constitute, and appoint the Agents, with full power of substitution, as my true and lawful attorneys in your name, and said Power of Attorney shall take effect on the date hereof and remain in effect in the event that I become disabled (as that term is defined in state law), to do each and every act which I could personally do.

If you have assets in more than just one state, you may need a durable power of attorney for *each* state. So if you own a vacation or winter home in a warm climate and a summer home up north, be sure you get a durable power of attorney in both states. They don't have to be identical—it's possible, for example, that they will name a different person to serve as agent or attorney-in-fact for the two different locales.

Guardianships and Conservatorships If you have no durable power of attorney but are unable to make a decision, the court may step in. If you are judged to be incapable of making your own decisions, the court will appoint a legal *guardian* who will have the authority to make decisions regarding living arrangements, medical care, and financial considerations. This guardian may be a relative, friend, attorney, or even an agency. The guardianship may be permanent or temporary, and the court may place limits on the powers of the guardian (for example, the guardian may be limited to financial decisions but not have authority to make health-care decisions).

A *conservatorship* is a type of guardianship that, in most states, limits the powers granted to financial affairs.

The key to having your wishes about these complicated matters take effect is to try to avoid having the court decide who makes decisions for you. By planning ahead, you can make sure your affairs are taken care of in the manner you would like, not necessarily what a court-appointed guardian may determine is in your best interest without knowing how you would want that decision made.

Living Wills (or Health-Care Instructions or Advance Directives) A living will, also sometimes referred to as a health-care instruction or advance directive, is a legal document that informs physicians, family, clergy, and all others of your wishes regarding your health if and when you become incapacitated and unable to make your wishes known. It usually specifies whether you do or do not wish to have your life artificially prolonged with the use of life-sustaining procedures or high-tech equipment if you have an injury, disease, or illness certified to be a terminal. It is a legal, binding document that tells doctors you give them permission—regardless of what other family members or friends may say—to, for instance, refuse all medical or surgical treatment and to permit you to die. You can direct the administration of medication to eliminate or reduce pain, and require that physicians and other health-care personnel remove all machines and halt all resuscitation. You can also specify whether you would want to be fed intravenously.

You can get a sample living will from a number of sources, including www.aarp.org/advancedirectives and estate.findlaw.com. Be certain to check with an attorney to make sure it is accepted in your state.

Some states will allow physicians to honor a person's wishes if they have made it clear to a number of people but do not have a written living will. But a written, legal document makes it much more certain that your wishes will be carried out.

Health-Care Proxy (or Health-care Directive or Health-care Power of Attorney) A health-care proxy is similar to a living will except that it is covers considerably more territory. Essentially it allows the person you select to be responsible for your health-care decisions in the event you are deemed incapable of making a medical decision (but are not necessarily terminally ill). It is a document that should be executed *in addition* to a living will. It may, in fact, turn out to be a more important document since health-care decisions are more often made when a person is *not* terminally ill.

A health-care proxy is quite similar to a durable power of attorney, but it does not require that an attorney draw it up (although it will require a notarized signature). Since health-care proxies vary greatly from state to state, it's best to get a form from your local hospital or county Area Agency on Aging.

Note

The Health Insurance Portability and Accountability Act (HIPAA) of 1996 set forth national standards for ensuring the security and privacy of health information. The health-care proxy should specifically authorize the person you select to access medical information, including any protected or individually identifiable health information, on your behalf. It is imperative that the health-care representative has access to medical records to be an effective surrogate decision maker. The specific authorization within the directive to release information to your representative will ensure the medical provider releases any and all information pertinent to your care needs.

Do Not Resuscitate (DNR) A do-not-resuscitate (DNR) order is an instruction to medical personnel that goes into your medical chart. It is most often found in the chart of a person who is in a hospital, nursing home, or other long-term care facility. People who have a DNR order in their chart have, in essence, instructed the medical personnel that they do not want any measures taken in the event they go into respiratory or cardiac arrest. Only a physician, not a patient or family member, can execute a DNR. This would be done in consultation with the patient, the health-care proxy, or family.

Goal #3: Making Sure There's Access to the Money

Achieving goal #3, ensuring that those responsible for your care, should it be needed, have access to your resources, is the natural step in the progression. It's one thing for someone to be able to make some decisions for you. But unless that person has access to your money, bills could go unpaid and, with regard to health care, you might not be able to receive the kind of care you'd want simply because no one has the authority to use the money you have set aside for this. In this section, I lay out a couple of ways to provide access to your finances.

Access to Assets Having easy access to your assets will be essential in making sure your financial obligations are taken care of according to your wishes.

As I mentioned earlier, one of the ways you can accomplish this is through a power of attorney. Though this document is perfectly legal, many clerks, tellers, and others with whom your agent will interact may be reluctant to rely on powers of attorney. As a result, using it can often be cumbersome and cause serious delays. In addition, many people balk at signing a power of attorney, fearing that they have lost control. In fact, they have not lost control, since the signer can withdraw a power of attorney at any time. Furthermore, the power of attorney document can limit powers, depending on how much responsibility or authority the signer wants to hand over. That is why most attorneys recommend this method of giving children access to parents' assets rather than simply becoming a co-owner of accounts or other assets.

A second way for someone to have access to your assets is through joint ownership. Most attorneys feel it is *not* as good a method as a power of attorney.

Simple Ways to Accomplish Access

- **Bank accounts**: Open a separate account with both you and your survivor having signature authority. You can designate either person as primary owner, which will affect who must claim any interest that's earned. Explore opening an agency or "convenience" account, which gives the other person access to the money without making him or her an owner of the money. If you meet resistance from others in the family, you can have multiple names on the account and require two signatures. You can then transfer funds into the account as needed, and transactions can be handled through check writing or through telephone or personal computer transfers. But be aware of any potential inheritance tax issues with multiple owners of assets. Joint ownership can also create potential problems if you need to become eligible for Medicaid benefits or the other owner gets sued, divorced, or has to declare bankruptcy.
- **Safe deposit boxes**: You should pick the one person you want to be able to get into your safe deposit box to access important papers and assets. This is critical if you become disabled

and are unable to go to the bank. Before there's a problem, you should go to the bank to add this person to the signature card.

- **Stocks and bonds**: Having easy access to your stocks and bonds is not quite as simple as just signing a signature card. For you to grant access to stocks and bonds means you are actually required to transfer them to new owners, requiring a signature guarantee or a transfer-on-death certificate that automatically transfers the asset when you die. Another easy way, other than having a power of attorney or transfer-on-death certificate, is to open a new account at a brokerage house in both of your names. You can then deposit or transfer the stock or bond into this account, giving the other person access. Since the new account has both names on it, there's usually no signature guarantee required.

Tip

Some brokerage accounts require signatures of all co-owners. Be sure to check when you open the new account.

Incapacity Most people remain able to make decisions for themselves until the day they die. Nevertheless, you can never be sure this will be the case for you, and your loved ones will certainly want to make sure you, or they, are making the best choices. The line between capacity and incapacity, however, may be unclear. Furthermore, people have the right to make their own choices, even if others consider them wrong.

But if there comes a time when you cross over the line and make choices that are harmful to yourself, you will want someone with the authority to step in. The very last thing you want your child to have to do is go to court to get you declared incapacited. Not only is it emotionally painful for everyone involved, but it also can be quite expensive. Before this last step becomes a necessity, discuss with an elder law attorney ways to avoid it. By taking the steps outlined above, you can avoid the legal and emotional difficulty as well as the expense of being declared incapacited.

Conclusion

In this chapter, I discussed transitioning your estate after you die. I explained the legal steps you should take to make sure your wishes are honored and, most important, your loved ones are taken care of as well as possible. Like some of the other chapters in the book, this one is a primer and should not be used as a comprehensive guide. If your estate or family situation is complex, you should speak with an attorney who specializes in estate planning to make sure what you've done will hold up in case there are any disputes.

It's always been worrisome to me when I hear about families who have not taken the legal steps necessary to protect their estates and their heirs. I'm especially concerned when there are minor children in the household. Beloved pets should also be provided for so they don't wind up in shelters when their owners die.

Ensuring a smooth transition of your estate, regardless of the size, is not only a smart thing to do, it's the *right* thing to do. You might think to yourself that because you have only two kids or everything is going to your partner, the transition will go smoothly. Maybe you're right. But something unexpected could crop up. Since it's so easy to take care of these details—and so relatively inexpensive—why take the chance? Following through and creating all the necessary legal documents may mean your family won't have to sort through a big mess.

Now that you've taken all these steps, it's time to focus on letting key people in on these important areas. In the next chapter, I discuss having "the talk" with your heirs.

CHAPTER

Have "the Talk" with Your Heirs

■ ■ ■

As I explained earlier, transitioning your estate begins with a conversation and ends with a plan: for your financial, insurance, and legal affairs, for your health, and for your wishes before and after death. Once you have a plan in place, the next step is to make sure the key people involved know the plan or, at a minimum, know how best to access the plan. Few of us are eager to talk about aging—and especially about death—but it's absolutely essential. The more you talk about these issues, the clearer it will be to those who may need to care for you what you want for yourself if and when you need assistance. In this chapter, I list all the areas you should discuss and offer answers to the following questions:

- What can you expect when you begin discussing your plans?
- Who should take part in the discussion?
- Who should be responsible for what?
- When is the best time to begin the discussion?
- How do you convey your wishes?
- Should your partner be involved?

Getting Started

As you begin these conversations with your survivors and trusted advisors, you may find that some topics flow from other topics, or that you are more willing to discuss certain subjects gradually. You may find to your surprise that you are quite comfortable talking about sensitive topics, even about your own mortality.

This is not to say that aging is an easy topic to discuss, especially with your children. But don't be too shocked if, when you begin to bring up the various subjects having to do with your own aging, you are much more comfortable than your children or survivors are. After all, you've had experience watching your own parents and other relatives and friends go through the aging process. Chances are you want for yourself a better life in later years than your parents or grandparents had. We need to make sure our children and others we trust know what our wishes are and understand as much as possible about our state of affairs.

That means you will have to confront your fears and think about your own mortality. You'll also have to confront the potential loss of control over your life, the interruption of the goals you had for yourself, the fear of being a burden on others, and the fear of surviving your partner, if you've had one.

Once you've faced these issues, the question will be, "How comfortable will my children be discussing these things?" Many children don't want to discuss these important matters with their parents, just as you probably didn't want to discuss them with your parents. Later in this chapter, I talk more about the responses you might get when you bring up the subject. But first, here's some advice about your initial approach.

Don't Assume

There's so much to cover about a person's state of affairs that it would be easy to miss or gloss over some areas because you assume they've already been dealt with.

The primary purpose of this chapter is to make sure you convey to your survivors the essential information they'll need so you'll be cared for as effectively as possible and your estate plans will be carried out. Some of the following material will be relevant to you; other areas may not apply. Try to address all the points I cover, since it's often the case that your children know less about your affairs than you think they do. For example, because your attorney is an old friend of the family, your children might reasonably assume that you have set up your papers appropriately, executed a proper will or trust, and signed a durable power of attorney, and that this friend of the family has all the documents and is the executor of your will. This could be an example of the shoemaker's children going without shoes. So, the primary rule is: Don't assume. Make it clear!

One word of caution: Keep in mind that when you discuss your financial and legal affairs, health concerns, housing, and wishes for after you're gone, you are giving your children more responsibility. Be certain they're prepared to accept this responsibility. If, for example, your children balk at talking with you about legal issues or your finances, you can encourage them to come along with you the next time you talk with your lawyer, accountant, or adviser.

Who Should Participate in the Discussion?

You might think that everyone who will have responsibility for you should either be involved in these discussions or, at least, be privy to the information that you share. But that's not always desirable or practical. You'll want to designate one person as the primary contact (or caregiver, if that becomes relevant). But it doesn't necessarily follow that everyone should be involved with all aspects, even the primary contact. If you and your family have decided to split up the responsibilities—that is, one child might serve as the executor and another as a potential caregiver—all parties should certainly know as much as possible about their immediate areas of responsibility. The person who will be making sure that all the legal and financial areas are covered should know as much as possible about your affairs, but that person need not necessarily be involved in handling some of the other day-to-day decisions of caregiving, if that should become necessary.

Splitting Up the Work

Although more and more families are working out ways to split up the duties and responsibilities, they are usually *not* equally shared. So the first thing you and your family must work out is who will be responsible for what. One of your heirs may serve as executor to your estate. One of your survivors may take responsibility for your health care, and so should be designated primary caregiver. More often than not, other than your partner, the first designated primary caregivers are women, while men more often take on the logistical and financial roles. I encourage you to make arrangements that will work out best for you. Generally, however, in most families, primary caregivers most frequently assume the role in this order:

1. The spouse.
2. The oldest daughter.
3. A daughter still living at home.
4. A daughter-in-law who lives nearby.
5. The son.

Ten Reasons to Talk with Your Children about Aging

1. So they can learn as much as possible about your current legal and financial affairs.
2. So they can learn as much as possible about your wishes, both before and after your death.
3. So you can impart information to them about your resources and about your health care and legal and financial affairs.
4. So you can help them, in the future, make decisions about your affairs.
5. So you can tell them about you and your life.
6. So they better understand factors that may have affected your relationship with them (or might in the future).
7. So they have a sense of heritage for them and their children.
8. So they can help you maintain dignity and as much control over your own life as possible.
9. So they can better cope with your aging and adapt to changes it will bring.
10. So they can talk about their feelings and reactions.

When to Have Your Discussion

A logical question is, "When should I have this discussion?" The quick answer is, "Now, because you can never have this discussion too early, and if you wait too long, it may be too late."

Discussing the future can help both you and your children prepare emotionally for the inevitable. You'll also be better able to ensure that your wishes are carried out. There are some logistical reasons for discussing your future earlier than you might have thought necessary. Of course, if you are reading this now, it is *not* too late.

Finding the Words

Remember that the purpose of your talk is to impart information, not to provide emotional counsel. So while this conversation often results in a discussion of feelings—and you will certainly want to be sensitive to and address those reactions—you ultimately need to focus on making sure your heirs have all the facts and plans. Whether that comes as a result of many discussions or a written response to a list of questions doesn't really matter. The goal is to provide comprehensive information and address all their questions.

If you and your children have a close relationship, live near each other or visit often, and talk about a variety of topics, you're probably in a fairly good position to discuss the issues of aging, estate planning, and inheritance covered in this chapter. You'll likely be able to discuss the changes you will undergo in your later years. But even so, starting that first conversation can be tough. Here I offer a few approaches:

- *The direct approach:* "I'd like to talk with you about the future. There are lots of things you need to know about. Is this a good time to talk?" or "When would be a good time to talk?"
- *Written approach:* "Here's an article/book/chapter I think might be good for you to read. I think it's really wise and helpful. After you've had a chance to digest it, I'd like to talk with you about what it says."

- *Third-party approach:* "I've been thinking about the future and have spent some time talking with my lawyer/accountant/adviser about my personal affairs. Would you be willing to have all three of us talk together?"

You may want to use a combination of these. Whatever approach or combination of approaches you use, pay attention to your children's lead. Appreciate how difficult it may be for them to talk and try to set aside old resentments.

Following are some typical responses and what you can say:

When they . . .	You might respond with . . .
Close off the conversation or change the subject:	"I'd like to talk about it, but I'll wait until you are ready." Then, be sure to bring it up again.
React with a strong emotional outpouring:	"I understand your reaction. Why don't we talk more when we're both ready?" Again, be sure to bring it up later. The level of emotion will likely subside.
Deny or reject the discussion:	"I understand your response. Still, it's very important that you know some things just in case something happens to me."

Be assertive about your desire to talk, but pay attention to your child's lead and to your own feelings and reactions. Often touching helps, as does empathy and active listening.

Important: Be sure to listen to their answers and be open-minded about their fears and concerns. When you express your wishes, remind them that they are *your* wishes. You can encourage them to express their own desires and feelings, and even try to persuade you to heed them if necessary. But remind them that people want to remain in charge of their own lives as long as possible. Unless you are in danger, you have a right to take risks and even to make foolish decisions about your own life. Remind them to treat you with the respect they would want for themselves.

Involve Your Partner

Traditionally, in our parents' generation, husbands handled most of the financial, legal, and "business" connected with the household, while wives dealt with the family and the home. In many households this is still the case. Therefore, major changes occur more often and cause potential problems when the husband dies, leaving the wife to take over. Some of these very capable women can handle the new responsibilities quite well, others not so well. This is not a statement about ability or a political ideology. The fact is that many of us fell more often into those gender-specific roles.

In some families the roles are reversed, and the wife has primary responsibility for household business affairs. If you are part of a family in which one partner is more in charge of those aspects than the other, make certain the other partner becomes fluent in the critical issues. When you have "the Talk" with your heirs, be sure both you and your partner are present and involved.

If you are in a blended family—that is, one made up of stepchildren and stepparents—it is even more important that the key people know all that they need to know. That can help prevent battles later on.

Top 10 Subjects to Cover during the Talk

Here are the top 10 subjects to cover and the information you must eventually provide or allow access to. The more thoroughly you address each issue, the better off your survivors will be when decisions have to be made. Some information is relevant to more than one category, and thus there is some overlap in the following list.

1. Home:
   - ☐ The name, address, and phone number of your mortgage holder, including second mortgages, and home equity loans or lines of credit.
   - ☐ The approximate balance of each mortgage.
   - ☐ If you rent, the monthly rent and security deposit paid as well as the name, address, and phone number of your landlord.
2. Health:
   - ☐ Your present condition (including normal blood pressure and cholesterol levels; dental health; normal degree and location of pain/discomfort).

☐ Long-term and short-term illnesses and your prognoses.

☐ Surgeries and history of any major illnesses.

☐ Allergies, especially if you are allergic to any drugs.

☐ List of current prescriptions with what they treat, who prescribed them, the frequency they should be taken, how long they are to be taken, and whether the prescription can be refilled (this will change often so using a computer spreadsheet will be most helpful).

☐ Degree of hearing and sight loss and last date both were checked.

☐ Usual complaints, such as frequent headaches, toothaches, dry eyes, dry mouth, fatigue, insomnia, arthritic pain, insomnia, sensitivity to cold (chilblains), constipation, or ringing in the ears (tinnitus).

☐ Inoculations (including the last flu shot).

☐ Names, address, and contact information of all the health professionals who currently care for you, including family doctor and specialists such as therapists, podiatrists, chiropractors, physical and occupational therapists, and optometrists.

3. Documents and other important items (with the location or copies):

☐ Birth certificates.

☐ Marriage certificates.

☐ Death certificate of spouse.

☐ Divorce decrees.

☐ Military discharge.

☐ Immigration and Naturalization Service card ("green card").

☐ Home deed and title or, if you rent, lease.

☐ Auto title, lease.

☐ Appraisals of valuables.

☐ Life, home, auto, and long-term care insurance policies.

☐ Disability and medical insurance policies and identification cards.

☐ Social Security card (or number)—your own as well as for all parents and stepparents, even if one has died.

☐ Burial-plot deeds.

☐ Wills and codicils.

- ☐ Living will.
- ☐ Trust.
- ☐ Power of attorney forms.
- ☐ Durable power of attorney forms.
- ☐ Health-care proxies.
- ☐ Advance directives.
- ☐ Home security system codes.
- ☐ Duplicate house keys.
- ☐ Duplicate keys to post office boxes.
- ☐ Duplicate car keys.
- ☐ Passwords for e-mail accounts, online banking and investing, credit cards, etc.

4. Insurance:
   - ☐ Private health insurance.
     - Kind of coverage.
     - Company name and address.
     - Policy number.
   - ☐ Health insurance identification numbers or cards.
   - ☐ Medicare/Medicaid identification number or the actual cards (number may be different than the Social Security number).
   - ☐ Medicare supplement (Medigap) insurance plans.
     - Kind of coverage.
     - Company name and address.
     - Policy number.
   - ☐ Long-term care insurance.
     - Kind of coverage.
     - Company name and address.
     - Policy number.
   - ☐ Life insurance.
     - Company name and address.
     - Agent's name, address, and phone number.
     - Policy number.
     - Amount of policy.
     - Beneficiary.
     - Cash value, if any.
     - The amount of any loans that have been borrowed against the policy.

☐ Auto insurance.
  - Coverage.
  - Company name and address.
  - Policy number.
☐ Homeowners or renters insurance.
  - Coverage.
  - Company name and address.
  - Policy number.
☐ Disability insurance.
  - Coverage.
  - Company name and address.
  - Policy number.

5. Religious concerns:
   ☐ Place of worship.
   ☐ Name of personal clergy.
   ☐ Wishes for a religious or nonreligious funeral service.
   ☐ Religious rules for handling of funerals.
   ☐ Religious beliefs as they relate to health care.

6. Finances:
   ☐ Names, addresses, and contact information of financial advisers.
   ☐ Names and addresses of all banks and other institutions with checking, savings, investments, and brokerage accounts, with account numbers and the names on each account.
   ☐ Complete list of assets.
   ☐ Complete list of debts and liabilities.
   ☐ Terms and balance of home mortgage.
   ☐ Property tax receipts.
   ☐ List of routine household bills (including mortgage or rent, utilities, insurance premiums, for example) and how they're paid (check, autopay, etc.).
   ☐ List of real estate holdings and rental property.
   ☐ Copies of tax returns for the last three years.
   ☐ Personal loan records (including loans made to family and friends).
   ☐ Open lines of credit.

- ☐ Location of safe deposit box and where both keys are kept; duplicate key and signature authority to access safe deposit box in institutions.
- ☐ Location and appraisals of valuables (jewelry, art, precious metals, silver, stamp and coin collections, etc.).
- ☐ Retirement and pension policies, with information on whether benefits are extended to the surviving spouse.
- ☐ Partnerships and interests in other business ventures.
- ☐ Credit cards (name, card number; current balance, and names on the account).
- ☐ Receivables from business or personal loans.
- ☐ Moneys set aside for funeral and health care.

7. Friends, relatives, and neighbors:
   - ☐ List of close neighbors, their addresses, and their contact information (including daytime phone numbers).
   - ☐ List of who has extra keys or access to your house.
   - ☐ List of friends and relatives who live nearby who can visit or stop in.
   - ☐ List of emergency contacts.

8. Plans for the future:
   - ☐ Wishes about housing arrangements.
   - ☐ Wishes regarding medical and crisis care and whether extraordinary measures are to be taken in life-threatening emergencies (advance directives).
   - ☐ Special holiday and birthday plans for family.
   - ☐ Funeral arrangements made, or wishes for a service.
   - ☐ Whether you want a burial or cremation.
   - ☐ If a cremation, what to do with your ashes.

9. Legal issues:
   - ☐ Name, address, and phone number of attorney.
   - ☐ Location of last will and testament plus all codicils.
   - ☐ Location and a copy of powers of attorney.
   - ☐ Location and copy of health-care proxy.
   - ☐ Deeds (home, burial plot, rental property, autos).
   - ☐ Birth certificates.
   - ☐ Marriage certificates.
   - ☐ Death certificate of spouse.

☐ Divorce decrees.

☐ Military discharge papers.

10. Personal contacts

☐ Associations, clubs, and fraternal organizations (many offer services and benefits).

☐ Veterinarian.

Life Story

My father was an attorney and, for the most part, made sure his affairs were in order, particularly as he got older. But while my stepmother was alive, he was very hesitant to talk about his finances with me or with my brother. There was friction in their household around money, and in my father's attempt to avoid controversy he hushed any conversation that might sound as if he was excluding her from participating in financial planning. True, he was more open when she was not around, but it was still difficult to find out as much as we needed to know, despite the fact that they had prenuptial and postnuptial agreements. After my stepmother died, my father was much more forthcoming and covered everything in the list I provide in this chapter that related to his situation with one glaring exception: He could not comfortably talk about life and death decisions. He couldn't say whether he wanted a do not resuscitate (DNR) order if his heart or breathing stopped, and he wouldn't sign a living will or health-care proxy. The subject was just too difficult for him. Fortunately my brother and I never had to face a decision about prolonging his life. Had we been forced to do so, my brother and I could never have been sure because my father was not clear. We can make it easier on our loved ones by being clearer, especially in areas we are uncomfortable discussing.

Conclusion

In this chapter I reviewed all the topics you need to cover when talking with your survivors or your trusted advisers about your wishes and about the business of your life. As these things change, you'll want to alert everyone and update the appropriate documents. To the extent you can be open and organized about these topics, you will make it easier for those following you.

The story about my father's later years illustrates the kinds of struggle we face when dealing with our mortality. But what stands out—and I suspect is not unusual, particularly in blended families like mine—is the unspoken concern about financial issues and how it relates to the degree of trust in the family. Those are areas you need to confront when you make your wishes known to your survivors. It won't be easy—finances and dying wishes are sticky points for many of us. In more complicated cases, you might prefer to confide in a trusted adviser outside your family. Just be sure you let your survivors know who that person is.

In the next chapter, I'll talk about your living arrangements, including the options you have and the decisions you will need to make.

CHAPTER

Home Sweet Home

■ ■ ■

Many of our parents bought their home when we were young, lived there most of their adult lives, and paid down their mortgages, sometimes completely. Although we left years ago, when we'd go to visit Mom and Dad, we still said we were "going home."

Many of us now can't relate to that quaint lifestyle of living in one home for so long. We've either moved several times or refinanced our mortgages to take advantage of declining interest rates so that it's become almost impossible to own our homes outright. One thing hasn't changed for those who have lived in their homes for a long time and raised a family there: When the kids who've moved out visit, they still say they're "going home." In some families the kids have moved back in (at least temporarily), so they can say "going home" and literally mean it.

My wife and I love that we have been able to provide that safety and security for our children and grandchildren. And we hope it continues. We also hope that our home remains safe and secure for us as we age.

But not all of us have that luxury. Some of us have lost our homes due to a bad economy, personal financial issues, or downsizing; some never had a house in the first place. After all, millions of people live in rented apartments quite happily, without a yard and white picket fence. Not everyone can identify with the people Norman Rockwell depicted in his paintings.

In this chapter, I focus on living arrangements. I discuss the options you have, the choices you will have to make, how your score on the level of activity scale influences those choices, and some of the outcomes or consequences, unintended perhaps, of those choices. I'll cover these topics:

- Empty nesters.
- Moving.
- "De-cumulation" and downsizing.
- Second homes.
- Adapting your home.
- Long-term care and assisted living.
- Living abroad.

Empty Nesters

Although the empty nest may seem like a relic in these days when children never seem to leave home or worse, go back as adults to live with their parents, most parents do get to experience it: that time when the last of the kids trots off to college or begins living on his own. It's a time that some of us anticipate with glee, others of us with dread, and others still with the mixed emotion of being on our own but yet missing the fact that we have no one to be responsible for.

It's natural to experience all the swings of emotion brought on by an empty nest. I encourage you to let go of any guilt that might creep into your subconscious for feeling the joy. That's easy to say, of course. But try—rather than denying it, and rather than thinking of yourself as a bad parent—to embrace the feeling. It's not as if you're abandoning your kid. You're simply feeling that you have more control of your life, now that the kids are not your every-day, every-minute responsibility. You'll still be there for them when they need you.

As for the dread, I suggest going back to Chapter 7, where I talk about how you will spend your leisure time. You'll think to yourself, "Oh my, the house will be so quiet. I won't know what to do with myself and all that free time." Exactly! For the first time in a long while you (and maybe your partner) will have time just to and for yourself. What a great time to think of all the possibilities. There are two points from the discussion in Chapter 7 that I want to emphasize:

1. Avoid any judgments about how you spend your time or whether what you are doing (or plan to do) is productive. You can take time to experience this new feeling and you don't have to explain yourself to anyone.
2. Pay attention to where you are and where you want to be on the level of activity scale. You'll want to use that knowledge to guide you in how you deal with your new leisure time and being an empty nester.

Moving

One of the biggest stress events for anyone is moving. I can't emphasize that enough. If you've ever remodeled your kitchen or had to give a speech in front of hundreds of colleagues or friends, take the amount of angst you felt then and multiply it 10 fold. Moving is so difficult on everyone involved that I suspect many people stay where they are not because they want to stay there, but because they loathe the idea of moving. In fact, most older Americans don't move.

Nevertheless, moving to another house or location is definitely one of the options you'll want to consider. Later in this chapter, I delve more deeply into some of the specifics about choosing the place where you'll live, but first, just think about what moving means. You're taking all your possessions, all your memories, and perhaps the lifestyle you've created for yourself over many years, and turning it all upside down. You'll get up in the middle of the night and not be sure which way the bathroom is. You'll hear new sounds (or stop hearing old sounds). Everything in your life will be different.

So even if the idea of chucking it all, getting out of your current rat race, starting over, and [fill in any aphorism you want] seems like a panacea, I encourage you to think long and hard about moving. Be honest with yourself and with your partner. Have numerous conversations about what it will be like, what you'll be giving up, and what you'll be gaining. You'll have many questions to answer and many decisions to make once you know all your options. If you still want to move, start thinking about the actual move itself. Discuss it with your partner, and go through all of the details—again.

Tip

Because of the enormous amount of stress you'll likely go through by moving, daydream about it first. Close your eyes and imagine yourself in your new locale. Be as detailed as possible: where do you park your car, how accessible is public transportation, where do you go, how easy is it to shop, what will visits from your family be like, how convenient will it be to see friends, and so on. But also, daydream about the actual move. Imagine yourself packing and unpacking, going through all your stuff, and making the decision to throw away or save things. This exercise will not only help you get a better sense of where you would want to move, but will reduce the stress of an actual move. In an odd way, envisioning throwing away those cherished tokens of your past will make the actual act of tossing memorabilia easier.

Where to Move

The most obvious thing you'll have to consider is where. You should think not just about a region of the country or specific geographic area, but be as specific as possible. In cities, for example, streets just a few blocks away are markedly different. So, when deciding where to move, be exact. That will make finding your new home easier. If you decide to work with a real estate agent—which I highly recommend—you will want to be able to explain exactly what you're looking for and where. The more details you can provide about your lifestyle and your desires about locale, the easier it will be for your real estate agent to find the right place. You may also want to look into Senior Real Estate Agents (www.seniorrealestate .com), who are trained to help people 50+.

Tip

I encourage using real estate agents when you consider buying or renting a new home. For the most part, sellers generally pay for the agent's commission, so you as the buyer essentially get free advice. If you decide to rent instead of buy, real estate agent's fees are most often taken from the landlord, not the renter. When looking for an agent, ask around; word of mouth can often lead you to a reputable one. Having a good rapport with your agent is important, so ask for a few referrals. Then you can decide with whom you are most comfortable.

When considering where you want to live, you don't necessarily want to limit yourself, particularly if you haven't spent a great deal of time in that area or if you haven't spent time there recently. The town or area of a city you used to love will likely have changed over the years. If you choose to work with a real estate agent, rely on that person's expertise.

If you've narrowed down the location to a few areas, you should find an agent in each, assuming they are not so close together that one agent knows all of the areas.

Where you are on the level of activity scale should be an important consideration in choosing your location. If you're an active person who is on the go all the time, you might prefer to live near a city where you'll have access to lots of activities and convenient transportation. You might not be content with a beach town, where the off-season is so quiet that the only live music you'll be able to hear is the ocean. You also must remember that by moving, you may have to give up some of the activities you once engaged in. If you had a bunch of pals with whom you socialized, played ball, went golfing, or had dinner parties, those lost opportunities may be difficult to replace.

Distance

There are two issues regarding distance you'll probably want to deal with when considering whether to move:

1. Distance from family and friends.
2. Distance from activities, services, and cultural venues.

Most of us like to be able to visit family and friends without traveling too far. We like to have them over to our house as well—and not always as overnight guests. So how far away you move will depend on how important it is that these people can visit you easily, or how easily you can get to them.

The second thing to consider about distance is how far away you will be from the activities you have been involved with for so many years. If you're accustomed to going out to dinner once or twice a week, and often to different restaurants, you'll want to be certain a new place will offer you the same kinds of options. A longing for Thai food will not be quenched by going to one of only two or three nonethnic restaurants in your new neighborhood. If you're used to going to museums, concerts, plays, and other cultural events, being far away from those venues will make you homesick after a short while. The notion of having to drive two hours late at night after dinner and a show might dissuade you from moving to a far-flung suburban or rural locale.

Tip

Don't underestimate the importance of being close to friends and family. For example, you may fall in love with a pastoral setting; moving there from your city life might fill a longing you've had all your life. But there may be a reason you never acted upon that feeling and left your old life behind. You've grown accustomed to your city way of life now, and making such a radical change will not be easy. Just the move itself will be a huge change. Having friends and friends nearby will be important in your adjustment. You also need to seriously consider how you will spend your leisure time. Equally important, you also need to consider how easy it will be to continue working, if that's what you decide to do.

Ten Questions to Ask Yourself about Moving

1. Do I like living where I live now?
2. What do I most like about it, and can I find that elsewhere?
3. Do I feel a need to move because of physical limitations? If so, can my current home be adapted for my needs?

4. Do I feel a need to move because of financial reasons? If so, are there other options, such as renting out a room or cutting expenses?
5. Do I want to live in a house with a yard that requires maintenance or a townhouse, apartment, or condo, where all outside work is handled for me? If I prefer a house, can I do all the maintenance required, or can I afford to hire someone else to do it?
6. How much living space do I want (not need, but want)? How many bedrooms do I need?
7. How far away from my current friends and family am I comfortable being? Will they visit, and would it be easy for me to visit them?
8. Do I want to live in or close to a city, in a rural locale, or in a suburb? Near water or mountains or hiking trails? If I prefer a city, will I use what a city has to offer? If I'm comfortable in the suburbs, is getting into the city easy enough by car or public transportation?
9. Is there a region in the United States I'm most comfortable living?
10. Would I consider living outside the United States? If so, what country?

Type of Housing

Equally important to you will be the type of housing you want. By "housing" I mean deciding whether you want to live in a private home versus an apartment, townhouse, or condo—or maybe in senior housing or a retirement community. Retirement communities are sprouting up in locations all over the country. And many offer various accommodations within the community: private home, attached duplex, apartment, town home, and so forth. Deciding what type of home you want will not necessarily limit your location.

The type of housing you choose will be greatly affected by where you are on the level of activity scale. If you have difficulty with mobility, you will want to make sure you don't have multiple floors to contend with, unless you also have an elevator. If you are active and like to garden or consider yourself somewhat handy, you may want to be able to set up your shop. Most town homes and condos have limited space for that type of storage.

"De-cumulation" and Downsizing

Remember George Carlin's routine about stuff? "All you need in life [is] a little place for your stuff. That's all your house is: a place to keep your stuff. If you didn't have so much stuff, you wouldn't need a house." It's his hilarious rant about stuff, one that will bring a knowing smile. Here's a link to an open version of the routine: http://baby boomerflashback.blogspot.com/2008/04/george-carlin-on-stuff.html.

As you think about your own stuff, and how you've continued to accumulate more and more, the notion of downsizing and, what I call "de-cumulation" may be attractive to you. First of all, when you do decide to take this step, you can pretty much decide to throw out the box full of stuff you never even opened the last time you moved! Most of us don't, of course. Instead, we move it to the next place and stash it with some new boxes of stuff that live in our basement or garage.

But the time may finally come when you decide you've had enough of those boxes and have stored enough memorabilia. As you think about moving, you'll need to decide not just how much of your stuff you'll want to bring with you but how much room you'll be comfortable allotting for it. If you don't have enough room now for the stuff you need to have, you won't be happy with the smaller amount of space you've thought about settling for.

Tip

Could you go from a 3,000-square-foot, four-bedroom home where your kids grew up to a 1,500-square-foot two-bedroom townhouse or condo? Really? Maybe. But unless your finances or health warrant such a move, you may not want to. Such a radical change can produce even more stress than a move normally brings. While it's enticing to think about not having to clean a large house or take care of a yard, downsizing is difficult, because many of us have gotten used to larger living space. If you're thinking about making that kind of change in your living arrangements, consider renting first for a short while to get used to living in smaller quarters.

Second Homes

George Carlin would have laughed about getting a second home so we could accumulate even more stuff! But, of course, the second home is not about having more but about having something different.

The number of people with second homes is a difficult statistic to measure because of the various reasons people have for owning real estate. But the U.S. Census Bureau estimated that in 2010 (the most recent survey data), more than 4.6 million living units were "used for recreational purposes." Although that number can include units that wouldn't qualify as a "second home" (for instance, they may be rental units where owners stay only occasionally or co-own with others), we still can be sure that a large number of people have second homes. There are even people who rent two homes, one for spring and summer and the other for the fall and winter, or some variation of that schedule.

Interested in this dual life? Here are some options:

- Own a vacation home strictly for your own use that you use on weekends, in particular seasons, or year-round for whenever you want to go.
- Own a second home that you stay in for no more than two weeks a year and rent out the rest of the year (making it an investment for tax purposes).
- Invest in an interval ownership home in which you are able to stay four weeks a year, generally one week per season (although trading with other owners is often done so owners are not always limited to one week at a time).
- Co-own a vacation property where you and a group of people (either strangers or people you know) collectively own and manage a property.
- Own a timeshare in which you can stay at the property for intervals of one week or can trade for other timeshares and similar properties (or can trade for points that can be used in hotels).

There are many advantages of each type of arrangement. There are also financial and tax implications for each. See Table 10.1.

Table 10.1 Advantages and Disadvantages of Owning Different Types of Second Homes

Type of Second Home	Advantages	Disadvantages	Comments
Vacation home (own use)	Can choose the house and location you want. Can go when you want, leave stuff there. Could be a way to try out as a place to live.	Most expensive option. Must furnish a second home. Must maintain from afar, although property managers can be hired.	May be the best option for pet owners. Beware: You may be the designated host for many family members and friends!
Part investment (can use two weeks)	More affordable because you can generate income and write off expenses. Can have an owner's closet for storage of personal items. Can try out as a place to live full time.	Limited to two weeks' use plus maintenance periods. Must also be a landlord or hire a property manager. Must find renters (more difficult and complicated with short-term vacation rentals). Legal and tax implications.	The tax issues are not difficult to manage, especially with tax software. Being a landlord can be difficult, time consuming, and stressful. Using online rental sites such as VRBO.com and homeaway.com can make finding renters easier.
Interval ownership	Often high-end properties for affordable price. No maintenance.	Limited to four weeks, one in each season (unless you trade). You're essentially paying for all seasons even though some weeks are not desirable.	In most locations, you wouldn't want to spend a week in certain seasons, and trading with others is not always so easy.
Co-own	Makes owning a second home affordable. Can share all expenses with other owners. Can trade usage times easily. Can try out as a place to live full time.	Limited use. Must arrange time with the other owners. Must handle maintenance or hire a manager.	Most groups assign a manager so it's not as difficult to coordinate. Many co-owners are flexible so you can trade or borrow time. But there can also be large expenses (although shared) and difficult owners!
Timeshare	Least expensive option. Often in resort areas. Can rent your week if you can't use it. Can exchange dates or resorts through companies like Interval International or RCI.	Limited to one week unless you buy multiple weeks or multiple timeshares. Annual maintenance fees can be high and you must pay even if you don't use the property. No resale value.	Weeks in good locations can often be rented for more than the maintenance fees through redweek .com or VRBO.com.

Adapting Your Home

If you've lived in your home for a long time—or even if you moved in more recently but love it—you may not want to move to a new place and leave your neighbors, friends, and activities. Or you may not be able to afford to move. In fact, 9 out of 10 people 65+ stay in their homes. As I said, moving can be one of the most stressful things you ever do, so staying put may be the most attractive option for you, even if circumstances seem to warrant moving. If, for example, you have a multistory home with the bedrooms upstairs and living space a flight down and you, your partner, or a parent who will move in with you begins to have more trouble navigating stairs, you might be considering a move. Similarly, if you have a home with a big yard that requires a great deal of maintenance and you don't want to continue doing all that work (and can't afford to pay for someone to do that maintenance), you might be considering a move.

But instead of moving, you can also consider adapting your current home to make it more accessible for you. In that way, you're not giving up your current lifestyle or moving away from friends and family.

Here are just a few ways you can adapt your current home to meet your current and future needs while avoiding the necessity of moving. Many of these options are low-cost ways to solve problems you may have with your current home.

- Add a bathroom with a standing, step-free step-in shower on the main floor.
- Add a master bedroom and full bath on the main floor.
- Install a ramp or a second entrance at ground level.
- Add railing for outside stairs.
- Add lighting (or increase the wattage of current bulbs, if safe) to make the house—and especially the stairs—brighter and easier to see.
- Convert an outdoor high-maintenance garden to a lower maintenance yard (replacing grass that needs to be mowed with ornamental grasses or rock garden).
- Install an intercom between floors, or use a phone with multiple handsets that can serve as an intercom.

- Add an intercom for the front door so you can talk to someone who rings your doorbell.
- Add handrails on stairs.
- In the bathroom, replace the regular tub with a walk-in, step-free tub or shower; add shower seating and slip-free surfaces; raise toilet seats; add grab bars; change to open shelving or add roll-out or pull-down shelves; increase lighting, including night lights or motion lights; lower counter height; add single-lever faucets.
- In your kitchen, use a side-by-side or French-door refrigerator to minimize bending down; install touchless or single-handle faucets; widen doorways, especially to a pantry; install roll-out or pull-down shelves and easy-to-grasp cabinet pulls.
- Remove or secure area and scatter rugs and use non-skid doormats.
- Add walk-in closets with accessible shelves and rollouts.
- Install an automatic garage door opener.

For more information about ways to adapt your current home, be sure to check out the Home Fit Guide available from AARP (www.aarp.org) and the *AARP Guide to Revitalizing Your Home,* by Rosemary Bakker, at www.aarp.org/RevitalizingYourHome. And visit www.longtermcare.gov or www.eldercare.gov, both sites of the U.S. Department of Health and Human Services.

When You Need More Help

I've often said that I can't fathom another move, so my next move will be into an assisted living facility, when I need assistance with my activities of daily living (ADL).

The fact is, as we age and as we move down the level of activity scale, we may need more assistance. It may be little more than a helping hand now and then, perhaps changing a light bulb that's hard to reach, moving a heavy table, or pruning a tree limb. Or maybe we need assistance walking up several flights of stairs to retrieve something we left behind, driving at night when there's glare and at dusk when the light is poor, or loading a heavy suitcase into the overhead bin. Inevitably, we will need more help. When the time comes that you or your partner cannot easily function in your home, and one or both of you need assistance more often than not, you may want to think about a different housing arrangement. The housing arrangement best suited for you will be determined, in part, by the degree of functional loss you or your partner is experiencing.

When insurance companies determine whether or not a person is entitled to long-term insurance benefits, they frequently rely on an index of eight activities of daily living: bathing, dressing, toileting, eating, transferring (mobility), managing medications, preparing meals, and housekeeping (see Table 10.2). You can use

Table 10.2   How Independent Are You?
Individuals are judged to be independent in the activity if they successfully perform the functions without supervision, direction, or active assistance.

Independent	Dependent
Bathing: washes oneself in either a tub or a shower, including getting into and out of the tub or shower, or by sponge bath without the aid of another person.	*Bathing:* needs assistance in bathing more than one part; not able to bathe self; needs assistance into and out of the tub or shower.
Dressing: gets clothes from the closet or drawers, puts them on, and attaches necessary braces or prostheses without the aid of another person.	*Dressing:* not able to dress oneself or only able to partly dress oneself.
Toileting: gets to and from the toilet and on or off the toilet and performs associated hygiene without the aid of another person.	*Toileting:* unable to get to and from the toilet, on or off the toilet, or perform associated hygiene by oneself.
Eating: feeds oneself by any means without the aid of another person.	*Eating:* needs to be fed by another person.
Mobility: walks without the assistance of a mechanical device such as a wheelchair, braces, walker, cane, or other walking aid device, and moves between bed and chair without the aid of another person.	*Mobility:* requires the aid of another person in walking, with or without the assistance of a mechanical device, and moving between bed and chair.
Managing Medications: takes medications in the prescribed amounts and at the prescribed times without the aid of another person.	*Managing Medications:* requires another person in taking medications in the prescribed amounts and at the prescribed times.
Preparing Meals: prepares complete, well-balanced meals without the aid of another person.	*Preparing Meals:* requires the aid of another person in preparing complete, well-balanced meals.
Housekeeping: does all routine housework, such as washing dishes or removing garbage, without the aid of another person.	*Housekeeping:* requires the aid of another person in doing all routine housework.

the same definitions to judge your degree of independence and the level of care you need. You might also take into account some other functions that, although they are not included in ADLs, are good predictors of the need for home care assistance, hospitalization, and institutionalization: shopping, driving, and managing personal finances.

The degree of independence you demonstrate and the level of care you need will determine whether you can adapt your home, need an aide come to your home to assist you, or should move to an assisted living facility or a full-care nursing home.

Living Abroad

No accurate headcount exists for the number of Americans who live abroad—the U.S. Census does not collect this data—but estimates are that about 6.3 million Americans live in foreign countries, excluding military. Obviously not all of these people are citizens, nor have all of them left the United States to retire or live out their senior citizenship in other countries. But clearly some have, and living abroad is definitely one option we all have when considering where to set up our home. In my travels, I have come across swatches of U.S. expats, as they are referred to, in nearby countries such as Mexico, Canada, and Costa Rica, but also in faraway countries like Australia or Japan. An expat (or expatriate) is merely someone who chooses to live outside the United States; it is *not* someone who disdains the United States (that's an expatriot). Some expats went to their countries of residence to work and just never left, or picked up their things and moved there for their retirement years. The number and variety of reasons for these moves is endless. My wife and I have often discussed living in another country, although we meant for a limited time, not for the rest of our foreseeable lives. And that's perhaps an intriguing way to think about the possibilities. With the Internet, Skype, and the communication systems that exist now—and allow us to stay in touch with our friends and family and conduct our business or manage our finances from afar—the move to a location thousands of miles away appears at first glance to be not that different than being in a different state.

But the fact is it's *very* different, and before heading overseas to live you should consider these areas where there are differences.

- *Culture shock:* No matter where you move, you will be in for a big change. Every place has a different way of life, a different speed, a different emphasis. Almost all expats experience a form of cultural shock, most mild, but some severe. The more you read about it, the more you learn about how life will be for you in a different country, and the more prepared you will be to handle the shock. Speaking with other expats will be an important part of your research.

- *Language:* In some countries, many people are bilingual or can carry on a conversation in another language. You may also get considerably more proficient in the local language in time. But being able to communicate will be important in developing relationships and also in emergencies or uncomfortable situations. Be especially careful about communication with health professionals if you are not totally fluent in the local language.

- *Finances:* Presumably if you are considering a move to another country, you will have taken stock of your finances and calculated how much income you'll need. But the whole tax structure is different in other countries. And some of the benefits that people in high-tax states enjoy don't extend to Americans living abroad.

- *Working:* If you are working for a U.S. company and will continue to do so, most of the issues you'll have to deal with will be worked out with your employer. If you plan to get some sort of work overseas or will work for yourself, you will have to thoroughly research the restrictions placed on you, both as a resident of the country and as a U.S. citizen. You should also understand all the tax implications of earning money in another country.

- *Health care:* One of the biggest reasons people give either for moving to a specific country or not is the health-care system and their own health. Any of us who are getting a bit grayer need to be conscious of health concerns, particularly those who are lower on the level of activity scale. So you should thoroughly research the health care that would be available to you as an expat and choose your location wisely. Different health-care systems have different requirements and pay scales. And your U.S.-based insurance may or may not cover you in other countries.

- *Housing arrangements:* In some countries and some areas you will have the same breadth of choice you have here in the United States regarding the type of housing you want. In other countries, that may not be the case. Again, research your options but consider not only what you might want or need now but also what you may need in a few years.
- *Pets:* Not all countries permit your pet to go with you, and some countries require a long period of quarantine. Be sure you have proof of all vaccinations and your pet's complete health history. Check to see that there's a vet nearby— particularly one with whom you can communicate if you're not fluent in the local language.
- *Single women:* It goes without saying that different countries and different cultures view women differently than they view men. If you are a single woman, you need to pay even more attention to both the obvious and subtle differences you can expect to experience. You should research this thoroughly and speak to single women in the country where you plan to move.

There are several good websites available for those considering moving to a foreign country, including www.internations.org, www .expatica.com, and www.transitionsabroad.com.

Conclusion

This chapter is all about your home: how some changes in your physical, financial, or family situation might lead you to move to another residence or another geographical locale, about the stress and other issues surrounding a move, and about the options available if you need assistance.

Clearly we can't always anticipate what the future will require of us. I never imagined that an accident would place some limits on my mobility. But I certainly knew that as I got older I wouldn't want to have to deal with as much house and garden maintenance as I had with my previous home. Parents can pretty much guarantee that eventually the last of the kids will move out (while hoping that some don't move back in). So an empty nest for those with children is likely. Those who do not have children won't have that kind of change thrust upon them. But they will have friends, relatives, and neighbors go through changes that force changes in their living arrangements and that will have an effect on everyone. The more you can anticipate the physical, financial, and emotional changes that occur in your life, the easier it will be for you to make appropriate choices about where you live. Similarly, the easier it will be for you to adapt to those changes if you plan for them. Most people have great admiration for those who rebound from adversity or go through difficult times and remain positive. A great strength that will serve you well is to embrace change, whether it was by choice or was thrust upon you.

In the next chapter, I talk more about the relationships in our lives: maintaining current ones and cultivating new ones.

CHAPTER

Relationships with Family and Friends

■ ■ ■

One of the most rewarding parts of getting older is the richness of the love and caring we share with our family and long-standing friends.

My wife maintained her friendship with Maggie since they were in third grade together. She always called Maggie her "oldest" friend. "Not oldest," Maggie would correct. "Longest standing." As the years flew by and the two young girls grew up to become women, they went to different colleges, settled in different parts of the country, got married, and had kids and grandchildren. They remained close friends, the relationship broadening to include a reservoir of family and friends. Such is the joy that comes with age.

Not everyone is so lucky to have had what these two women had. When we lost Maggie to cancer, we became much more aware of how important people are to us, and we began to think a bit more about what our own lives have meant or could mean to others.

In this chapter, I talk about the kinds of relationships you may have with family and friends and about these issues:

- Leaving a legacy.
- Remarriage.
- Singles.
- Caregiving.
- Pets.

Leaving a Legacy

We all want to be remembered and we all want to feel we have contributed something to the world. For some, of course, this can be a driving force leading to great accomplishments and extraordinary contributions to humankind. I always wondered how people could be so driven that they would consider running for the presidency of the United States. Sure, there's likely some egotism involved. But the commitment is so enormous that anyone willing to take on that responsibility has to do so for a lot more than just egotism. I think that what pushes many of us to achieve is the desire to leave a legacy.

Note

Legally, a legacy is a gift of property given through a will. But the broader definition would include anything handed down from the past. It is this characterization that most people think of when considering their own legacy. The two concepts are related and can be combined through the use of "ethical wills" or similar documents.

What do I mean by a legacy? Certainly it can include financial resources. But it's so much more. It's putting your stamp on the future. It's a way to make some meaning of and for your existence. "Yes, world of the future, I was here. Here's my contribution, here's what I stood for, and here's why I hope my life mattered."

You can leave a legacy in many ways. Through your last will and testament or trust, you can leave money or property to your survivors. Presumably that will make a difference to them. Your granddaughter might someday set her dining room table with the precious china you bequeathed her, that same china you got from your grandmother. Her children will know that it's been in the family for many generations. And each chip in a dish will signify a moment from the past.

But your legacy is not just about material things. Your nephew will be teaching his son how to fish, and as he explains the feel of pulling up on the rod, he'll flash back to the time you taught him that same technique. That's also a legacy. In fact, most of what we leave our children and grandchildren are memories—of who we are and of what mattered to us. As the old saying goes (oft cited with different credits and oft adapted), "There are two things we can give our children. One is roots; the other is wings." Your legacy takes the roots deeper, providing an even stronger foundation for them to branch out.

We provide this legacy by being with our loved ones and through our relationships. They pick up who we are by observing us, just as we learned from others. We become role models for the next generation. That's an enormous responsibility but, fortunately, one most of us relish. It brings meaning to our lives.

Life Story

Mark and Julia never had children in their 35-plus years of marriage. But they consider themselves blessed to have had close relationships with their nieces and nephews. Although they were not part of the early, everyday lives of their nieces and nephews, events conspired to draw Mark and Julia closer to two in particular. When the father of those two left the family, the children's relationship deepened with Mark and Julia. And when the youngsters grew up and had their own families, Mark and Julia were as tightly connected with the families as any parent or grandparent could be. As Mark and Julia considered their legacies and their wills, the niece and nephew and their respective spouses and children were significant recipients and beneficiaries. But equally important, the families reassured Mark and Julia that they would be taken care of in their old age, relieving the couple of much stress and concern for their own future.

We can do more than just be a good role model. That implies some passive role through which our children see who we are and emulate us. Instead, we can take a more active role. Here are a few ways we can do that.

Providing a Family History

Earlier, when talking about ways to transition from working full time to filling your time with various challenging and stimulating activities, I talked about researching your family tree. What a wonderful way to leave a legacy. By using all the tools now available, you can research your family as far back as possible, thus providing a foundation for your children and grandchildren to fill in gaps and add to this history. A good resource for this is AARP's *Genealogy Online: Tech to Connect* (John Wiley & Sons, 2012), aarp .org/AARPGenealogyOnline.

When you then add your own personal story by writing your memoirs, you will enrich the mere facts and provide fullness and color. As I suggested, be sure to include anecdotes and feelings so your heirs and survivors can know not just the facts of your life but also what it felt like to live during those years. Describing and illustrating your relationships with your parents and grandparents, aunts and uncles, siblings, and children will provide a legacy that no one else can provide.

Charitable Giving

We can contribute money or the equivalent to a charitable cause that reflects our values. The wealthier among us can create a foundation or create a trust that provides ongoing distributions so that the gift has more lasting value. For example, you can create a scholarship to your alma mater for future students. Most colleges have development offices to help you set up this program. Many require at least $25,000 to create an ongoing trust, but that money doesn't have to go to them right away; it can be left in your will, for example, to go to the school or organization after you die. Charities and colleges can also create annuities under which they are designated as the beneficiary when you die, but during your lifetime the annuity pays you from the interest it earns, like any other annuity. The difference is that you get a tax credit for some of the donation. After you die the proceeds belong to the charity or college. As with any financial investment—and indeed this is an investment, not just a donation—you should thoroughly review the terms and conditions. And you should check with your tax and financial advisers to make sure it is the right program for you and the best way for you to accomplish your financial goals.

The "Letter"

Think about everything you would want to tell your loved ones and your survivors if you knew you didn't have long to live, and then put that in a letter. You obviously would want to make sure the executor of your will knows everything he or she needs to know about the business of your life—that is, things like your Social Security number; the location of your bank accounts, insurance papers, deeds, and so on; and your passwords to accounts. That way, when that proverbial bus hits you, your survivors are not scrambling around trying to get everything done, *when they themselves are mourning*! So even if you don't have a will or trust, *someone* needs to know the real basics. You have to explain a lot of the details of your life: what you want done with your remains, whether you want a memorial service, where your legal documents are, and what your user names and passwords are. Here's a list of things

Warning

It's critical that someone know about the business of your life: your Social Security number, insurance information, bank accounts, investments, and so forth. Those things are often not specified in a will because they change so often. So whether you have a will or not, you should write a letter to your survivors, detailing everything they will need to know when you die. Even if you don't want to write any of the personal messages to your loved ones, or don't feel capable of doing so, at least make sure you detail your business affairs and explain your wishes for a funeral or service so that your survivors don't have to guess. But don't wait! This is one of those critical tasks that doesn't require too much work but can have a huge impact if left undone. No one wants to imagine the end of his or her life, particularly while relatively young. But sometimes things happen unexpectedly and your children and other survivors will be so much better off if you take just a few simple steps and write your basic letter to them.

you want to include in your letter to your survivors and the executor of your will.

Some Things Your Survivors Need to Know

- Your full legal name.
- Your Social Security number.
- Date and place of your birth.
- Date and place of your marriage and date of divorce (if applicable) and location of legal papers.
- The location of your original will or trust.
- The executor of your will.
- What you want done with your remains.
- Instructions for a funeral or memorial service.
- Newspapers where you wish to have an obituary.
- Religious affiliation.
- Veteran status (dates of enlistment and discharge).
- Whether you are an organ donor.
- Location of your legal documents (deeds, mortgages, insurance policies).
- Your insurance agent or company (life, health, auto, long-term care)
- User names and passwords to websites (e.g., bank, mortgage, credit card) or where user names and passwords can be found.
- Bank accounts and the location of checkbooks.
- Safe deposit box, location of the key, and who already has access.
- Location of any investments, including retirement accounts, and the name of and contact information for your adviser.
- Name of and contact information for your attorney.
- Location of previous tax returns.
- Names and addresses of your family and close friends (or where this list is located).
- Professional and fraternal organizations.
- Additional instructions or comments.

That last item is what makes this letter special. Here's where you get your chance to speak directly to your loved ones and say all those personal things you wished you could have said earlier. You can tell your grandson what it meant to you to be at his birth and to hold him just moments after he took his first breath. And how sad you would be if you won't be able to watch him grow. You tell your partner about the joys your relationship brought to you and how you hope that after you're gone, he or she carries on and finds happiness, even if it means with another partner.

Ethical Wills

With an origin going back centuries of elders orally conveying their values to the next generation, the ethical will is the logical extension of the "Letter." As opposed to other types of wills—a last will and testament or a living will—an ethical will is a nonbinding document in which you have your chance to share the meaning of your life, your beliefs, and your life's lessons. There are no rules governing it since its use is not about your possessions and how they get distributed to your heirs, although it can very well be about why certain possessions are distributed to specific people. An ethical will can be in writing, an aural recording, or on video; it is your way of telling your personal story. It's not your memoir, although certainly some facts about your life can and should be included. Rather, it ties together what you did, how you lived your life, and what you hope your heirs will take from you. It's your way of still being in the room.

Your ethical will is different from your last will and testament and your "Letter." You're not telling your heirs or survivors where your papers are or how you want your remains treated. Instead you begin by asking yourself, as Susan Turnbull, founder and principal of Personal Legacy Advisors says, "What is the most important thing you would not want left unsaid?"

Your ethical will can include pictures. In fact, it can be almost like a scrapbook with pictures and anecdotes, perhaps of you and your child at a significant moment in her life, next to which you jot down a paragraph explaining what that moment meant to you. For example, the note next to the picture of your daughter graduating from college can be something like, "With Julia at her graduation. It was at that moment, Julia, that my heart overflowed with joy. I saw then how good you felt about yourself after all your hard work. The 'Thanks, Dad' meant so much to me, more than you could ever imagine."

Several excellent resources can help you understand and write your own ethical will. Among them are *Ethical Will Book—The Wealth of Your Life* by Susan Turnbull (www.yourethicalwill.com) and *Ethical Will: Putting Your Values on Paper* by Barry K. Baines, MD (www .ethicalwill.com).

Remarriage

The U.S. National Center for Health Statistics (*Vital Health Stat 23(22). 2002.1*) estimates that over half of divorced men and over 40 percent of divorced women in the United States get married again. In addition, the U.S. Census reports that of all married people in the United States, about 20 percent are in at least their second marriage. So with more than 56 million households made up of married couples, we can safely say that of all adults, more than 20 million people have remarried. And this does not even include the number of unmarried couples who are in their second or more serious relationship. With so many of us living in second, third, or subsequent marriages or relationships, there are some key things to talk about here, including prenuptial agreements, postnuptial agreements, and finances.

Prenuptial Agreements

The complexity of each situation is unique. And in dealing with the ramifications, you'll want to consider a multitude of questions such as whether there are children involved, whether these children still live in the household, the degree to which the divorced spouse remains involved with the kids, and the expected role of the step-parent. Because of the nature of these issues, signing a prenuptial agreement before you remarry is highly recommended, especially if you have children or a complex financial portfolio.

When starting a new relationship, the last thing you'd ever want to bring up is the idea of having both partners sign a contract spelling out their rights and the limitations. It's contrary to everything we want to establish in this new marriage. It says, in effect, "I don't think this is going to last, I don't trust you, and I need to protect myself, my family, and my possessions."

Nothing could be further from the truth. You don't buy car insurance because you think you're going to have an accident. You buy it because you *might* have an accident and it's the responsible thing to do so you don't have unlimited liability if something catastrophic happens. Same with health insurance.

I view prenups as a kind of insurance policy. A good prenup does spell out rights and limitations and is a legal, binding contract. But it doesn't in any way say you don't trust your new partner or that you don't believe the relationship will last. Let's face it, stuff happens, and we can't always anticipate everything.

Ten Requirements of a Prenuptial Agreement

1. Specify who the partners are.
2. Disclose all the property interests of each partner, including real property, investments, pensions, and retirement accounts.
3. Specify the value, liability, and obligation of each property interest.
4. Explain in detail what is to happen with each property in the event that the partners dissolve their "partnership."
5. If either partner has minor children from a previous relationship, specify what rights are given to the other partner.
6. Explain what will happen if the partners have a child.
7. State that the contract is binding and whether binding arbitration would decide any dispute.
8. Include any legal requirements specific to your state of residence.
9. State the period of time this prenup is valid (to prevent sunset clauses).
10. Have partners sign the document, and have both signatures notarized.

Some very good websites can provide templates and sample prenups on which you can base yours. Check out www.prenuptialagreements.org and http://family.findlaw.com/marriage/sample-premarital-prenuptial-agreement.html. Be sure that any prenup you use is valid in your state and, of course, since this is a legal, binding contract, check with your attorney.

Tip

Prenuptial agreements may be valid only for a specific period of time. Some states have sunset clauses, after which the agreement is no longer valid. In addition, if the family structure changes—for example, you have a child—the prenuptial agreement may no longer be in force, since children have legal rights as heirs. Be certain you address these concerns by checking with legal counsel and updating your agreement accordingly.

Postnuptial Agreements

If you don't have a prenup, and get remarried or have a new partner, you should consider writing a postnuptial agreement. It doesn't matter when you and your partner work out an understanding, as long as you do.

As I said above, stuff happens; things change. And if both parties are agreeable, there's no reason a prenup can't change too. It happened with my father and his second wife. It worked out a lot better for everyone. In that situation, they had agreed in the prenup to something that wasn't realistic or fair. It had to do with the disposition of their home after the second one of them died; they had mistakenly used an actual number, not a percentage, when calculating how the property would be divided among the stepchildren. It made much more sense to amend what they had agreed to earlier.

That certainly was a simple fix. Since the parties were in agreement, they wrote up a new contract, called a postnuptual agreement, signed it, had it notarized, and notified the executors of their will and all the beneficiaries that this new agreement superseded the prenup. It's done all the time and, in fact, highly recommended. Imagine that you have a child in your second marriage. By law that child has specific rights as an heir. To have him not be a part of any agreement would actually nullify the prenup.

Similarly, if your prenup doesn't deal with a new grandchild but addresses all of the other grandchildren, it would likely be thrown out if contested. Clearly, in that case the prenup should have addressed grandchildren as a whole, not specifically. But if it doesn't, you must come to a new agreement.

In addition to births, a lot of other scenarios come about over time, such as change or loss of jobs and change in housing, health, and assets. One huge change might be when one of the partners inherits some significant property. Since the prenup might not have dealt with that property, you would be remiss to not revisit it with a postnup.

Notes

Prenuptial and postnuptial agreements are legally binding contracts that reflect your wishes for your property. They're not much different than a last will and testament and, as such, should be revisited to make sure they're still relevant and makes sense. If not, and if both parties can agree, revise your existing agreement according to both of your wishes. Then make sure it states clearly that it supersedes any previous agreement.

As always, you should check with your attorney to make certain the postnuptial agreement complies with your state laws and, most important, reflects what the partners want.

Singles

The number of households in which one person lives alone is remarkably high—the U.S. census estimates that in 2010, more than 30 million adults lived alone, equal to over 25 percent of the total number of households. More than 9 million of these people are over 65 years old.

In this section, I'm talking about people who are single in the legal and nonlegal sense, and what that means. The fact remains that when you're not in a long-term, committed relationship, life is different and you face very different issues. And if you're not legally married, you'll face even different issues. Throughout this book, I have tried to point out those differences and how you deal with them.

These differences are reflected in your finances, health insurance, estate planning, housing, leisure time, travel, and, in fact, just about every facet I have covered in this book. If you just look at one aspect of the legal world, what to do with your estate when you die if you don't take care to have a will, that is, you die "intestate," there are no specific guidelines as to how your estate will be disposed of if you are single. Unlike married parents, you don't have any automatic heirs. An executor or court will almost always automatically award estates to the children of people who die without a will.

If you get sick and are hospitalized, many times only "family" is allowed to visit. The definition of family might be broad, but being simply a friend will not necessarily permit access. More importantly, the hospital will tell family, but not a friend, anything about your condition. This might be unfair and arbitrary, but privacy laws prevent them from disclosing anything about your condition. So you must take specific steps to deal with the fact that you are single. In states that recognize legal unions or gay marriage, some of the concerns will be alleviated for those "singles" in relationships. But if you travel to a state that does not recognize your marriage or legal union, your partner may not have the rights granted in your home state.

Warning

Not all states recognize legal unions or gay marriages, even if your home state does. If you and your partner are traveling in a state—or country— that does not recognize your legal status, you may not have the rights you assume you have. In these cases, it is especially important that you take legal steps to avoid difficult situations such as if you are hospitalized. If you are in a legal union or gay marriage, you should speak with an attorney about what you can do—or what documents you can take with you—so that your legal rights are not challenged.

Caregiving

The fact that there are more than 9 million people living alone who are at least 65 years old is the perfect segue into the subject of caregiving. It is a topic with which I am personally quite familiar. I refer you to my book *How to Care for Your Aging Parents* as a resource and to my website, www.BartAstor.com. There are many other wonderful books on the subject. AARP has terrific information as well, including the AARP Caregiving Resource Center at www.aarp.org/caregiving, the *AARP Guide to Caregiving* e-book at www.aarp.org/GuideToCaregiving, and *Caring for Your Parents: The Complete Family Guide*. And especially I direct you to a book written by Gail Sheehy, who wrote the Foreword to this book. Gail wrote a compelling book on the subject, *Passages in Caregiving—Turning Chaos into Confidence*, available online and in bookstores. You can learn more about her at www.GailSheehy.com.

Whether you're dealing with an aging parent or a partner, the issues are mostly the same and—having been through it multiple times—I know they can be painful and difficult to deal with.

Key Points about Caregiving

- You are not alone. More than 52 million people in this country are caring for their parents or spouses. Rest assured (interesting words to use in this case) that you share common concerns and difficulties with many people.
- Reach out to others. Even mentioning something to a friend or colleague will elicit stories, questions, and support that you may not have expected but are helpful.
- Contact support organizations such as Children of Aging Parents (www.caps4caregivers.org), Today's Caregiver (www.caregiver .com), and Lift Simplified Caregiving (www.liftcaregiving.com) that can provide you with support, specific guidance, resources, and helpful tips.
- Organize and plan. Staying on top of things will be difficult because so much will be changing rapidly. But to the extent you can organize all the "administrivia" involved, the better off you and the person you are caring for will be. As a plus, when you are organized, you'll probably feel considerably less stress and anxiety.

- Take care of yourself as a caregiver. It's easy to burn out. The stress is high, the demands endless, and the emotional output draining. If you neglect yourself, you'll be less help to the one you are caring for.
- Don't do it alone. I can't emphasize this enough. Involve your family and friends in any and every way possible. Just because a sibling lives far away doesn't relieve them of the obligation to care for your parents. There are many things people can do from a distance.
- Don't feel guilty. Sure, that's easy to say. But feeling guilty is a value judgment, and I hope that you've seen by now that I don't believe in judging what we do or who we are. We do what we can because we want to. To scold or berate yourself does you no good. Using guilt to motivate others, on the other hand—an uncooperative sibling, for example—may work. At least on a short-term basis. I'm not advocating that, but if it helps get that person involved, I will generally advocate doing what you have to do to make sure the person you are caring for gets the best care.

Losing Friends

My father and stepmother died when they were in their 90s and 80s, respectively. My family mourned, but we also accepted that they had lived long lives and we knew they would ultimately die. The same is true of older aunts and uncles. It hurts to lose an older loved one, but it's expected.

Then, at some point, if you haven't already experienced it, you lose a friend or relative who is the same age as you. Then there's another one, and another one. You see friends coming down with illnesses that only your older relatives had—adult onset diabetes, cardiovascular disease, prostate cancer. It's part of the aging process and also the fact that we know more people who are older and more susceptible to these illnesses. For most of us, when we see death or illness affect our peers, we count our blessings and try to be as supportive as we can. You may feel extremely sad for a while, perhaps crying and feeling depressed. You may feel moody, angry,

192

or even guilty, as if there's was something you could have done—or guilt because you're okay and your friend is not. Often there's the fear that it will happen to me. After all, we're the same age.

Having gone through these losses all too many times, I take comfort in knowing there was nothing I could have done other than feel the pain of those who were close to the one who's gone, sympathize, and listen as they express their grief.

Tip

One of the greatest gifts we can give our friends who have lost a loved one is active listening—in particular, showing nonverbal reactions such as nodding your head, making eye contact, and leaning in. These cues make it clear that you are engaged and interested without interrupting as your friend expresses feelings.

Of course, I know I will have feelings of emptiness and loneliness, having lost someone close. I also know that these are normal reactions and unless they continue for a long time and interfere with our lives, they are not something to be alarmed about.

But for some, it's more serious. Below are some of the symptoms you might observe—in yourself or others. When the grief is severe and lasts a long time, it might be appropriate to seek professional help, whether therapy or a bereavement group.

Typical Symptoms of Grief

- Loss of appetite for more than a few days.
- Fatigue.
- Sleeplessness.
- Nightmares.
- Headaches.
- Excessive crying.
- Forgetfulness.
- Excessive use of alcohol or drugs.
- Feelings or talk of suicide.

Pets

This may seem like an odd subject to include in this book. I do so for a couple of reasons, the first being the love I have for my own pets, our two wonderful border collies. They are members of our family. We hope our older guy, who's now 11, has many more years and that his sister lives a long life too. I can't imagine not having taken appropriate steps to ensure they are cared for if something happens to me and my wife.

The other reason for including this topic is the staggering number of people who own pets and the effect pets have on our health, finances, estate planning, leisure time, and travel.

Some key statistics from the American Pet Products Association National Pet Owners Survey:

- More than 70 million households have pets! *Seventy million.* That's 62 percent of all households.
- There are over 377 million pets in the United States. Admittedly, 160 million are fish that are easily cared for. But there are 86 million cats, 78 million dogs, 16 million birds, and 8 million horses.
- Americans spend, are you ready, $53 billion on their pets annually, including more than $14 billion on veterinary care.

With numbers like these, we simply cannot ignore the fact that the roadmap to the rest of our lives may include a pet. Let's look more closely at the roadmap discussed in this book and see where pets fit in.

- *Finances:* With Americans spending more than $53 billion every year on pets, that equates to about $750 per household per year. That may not be a particularly high number for most families, but it's also not insignificant. I venture to say that the expenditures of fish owners bring that average way down. In fact, looking at just dog and cat owners, the survey shows that dog owners spend an average of double that amount, $1,500, per year and cat owners spend $1,200 per year. Keep in mind that's an average, with the average vet bill being only about $650. I know for a fact that my vet bill is much higher, just for routine care on two dogs. We've been fortunate that we haven't had other vet bills for more serious conditions, at least not recently. But when something happens to our beloved dogs, we will have no trouble insisting that they get the care they need; we will go as far as we can to pay for the appropriate care. We know people who have spent thousands on surgeries, chemotherapy, and even artificial joints. Although there is medical insurance for pets, those plans are expensive and have limited coverage (including an exclusion for preexisting conditions). Still, for some it's a good investment and you can investigate these medical plans through your own vet. The important point to make here is that you should be certain to include your pet expenses when preparing your budget, particularly as your job status and income changes.

- *Estate Planning:* My wife and I have made arrangements with close friends who have agreed to take our two dogs in the event we die. In addition, we have set aside a small pot of money—enough for at least a year or two—for their care. And we specify in our wills that if these friends need more because of unusual expenditures for the dogs, our executor will provide it from our estate. We will also revisit our wills periodically and will make it a point to do so when anything changes regarding these two wonderful four-legged family members. As a responsible pet owner, I hope you'll also take the necessary steps to make sure that your pets don't wind up at a shelter.

- *Leisure Time and Level of Activity Scale:* Border collies require a great deal of time—they're not the kind of animals who will sit at your feet all day. But I make it fun for all of us. In fact, as I explained in the opening chapter, because where I am on the level of activity scale has changed, I have had to re-imagine ways to compete in athletics. I now engage in the sport of dog agility. We train and enter competitions, thus fulfilling my need and strengthening the relationship with my dogs. The point here is that responsible pet ownership requires spending time with your pet. Some of us spend more time and energy, some less. And this changes over time. It also changes depending on where you are on the level of activity scale. It is a part of our leisure time affected by the LOA scale.

- *Travel:* We have been fortunate that our two dogs are able to stay with their nanny, who loves our pups as she does her own. Most pet owners are not so lucky, and if they go away they either have to take their pets, board them in a kennel, or find someone to come visit or live in their home while they're away. That certainly adds to the expense of travel, and you will always want to build that amount in when you're calculating the cost of the trip. Many people take their animals with them—most dogs travel well, cats not so well but they do travel—and stay in hotels that permit pets. Many people choose RVing to be able to have their pets with them. In addition, more and more quality hotels accept pets, usually for an additional fee. Furthermore, you may find networks of animal sitters in your hometown and in places you are visiting. You can do your own Internet search, but two good sites I have found are www.dogfriendly.com and www.officialpethotels .com. When traveling by air with your pet, be certain you know the airline's rules, regulations, and costs. When traveling by car, I hope you'll be extraordinarily careful about the safety of your pets, just as you would for your children.

- *Health:* Lastly, there should be no doubt in anyone's mind that having a pet can improve your health. Studies have repeatedly shown there are great benefits. In fact, the Centers for Disease Control website states, "Pets can decrease your blood pressure, cholesterol levels, triglyceride levels, and your feelings of loneliness." It goes on to say, "Pets can increase your opportunities for exercise and outdoor activities and opportunities for socialization." We have seen therapy dogs that lift the spirits of the depressed and service dogs that visit the infirmed, providing much relief and reward. My own pets often lift my spirits and provide me with companionship and unqualified love.

Conclusion

In this last chapter I covered a lot of ground about a variety of areas: our legacy, our message to future generations, caring for our loved ones. I dealt with the relationships we have with others and how we are trying to do the right thing. In a sense, we are trying to provide the best for those we care about and be the best we can be.

I concluded this chapter with a discussion about pet ownership. My two dogs remind me every day and in every way that they're not human, they're dogs. As John Steinbeck said about his dog, "Charley feels he is a first-rate dog and has no wish to be a second-rate human." That provides me with solace and inspiration. I don't need to be anything but what I am. And I continue to strive to be a first-rate human on the roadmap for the rest of my life.

Afterword

This book is about preparing for your Second Adulthood, as Gail Sheehy so eloquently wrote in the Foreword. At this point in our lives, as she notes, there are no more "shoulds." Although our parents may still be around—and some of us may be caring for them as they are aging—they don't have the same influence on our choices as they did when we were under their roofs. Maybe it would be a good thing if they did have more influence—perhaps their wisdom and experience would help us. But presumably we're all a bit older and wiser now, so we determine the "shoulds." We've made our choices, and we've lived with them for many years. We've accepted that they were, in fact, our choices. We chose whether to have a family, where to settle, what kind of work we would do, and what would occupy our time when we weren't otherwise overwhelmed with work and family commitments. We probably set goals for ourselves, and the goalposts may have shifted more than once. We saw others around us whom we admired, and we tried on what we saw in them. If those characteristics fit us, we took them on as ours. That's not any different than what our parents and their parents before them did.

But life was different for them. Their lives—at least from my perspective—seemed more predetermined. My mother didn't have the same options that my granddaughter has. Even as my wife was growing up, she was expected to be a teacher or a nurse, if she worked at all.

As our society changed, we found that we had more freedom. And with that increased freedom came uncertainty. With fewer role models and with changing goals, we stumbled on our way as best we could.

So it is with our next chapters in life. Who's in front of us? Who's clearing our paths? Gail Sheehy called this a book for those who don't want to be victims. I can't think of any better way to describe what I tried to communicate or, for that matter, what drives me today.

Sure, sometimes life brings the unexpected—illness, injury, or lottery winnings. But more often than not, we see the ball coming at us right off the bat. As it heads our way, we generally don't have time enough to consider all of the options. We needed to have thought about them before the ball was pitched: What if the ball is hit to me? Where do I throw it? Who's on base? How fast is the runner?

Then I let my muscle memory take over as I scoop up the grounder and throw it to second base to start the double play. If I bobble it, that's an error. Errors happen; we do the best we can. If I don't know what I'm supposed to do with the ball when it comes to me, that's more than an error. That was preventable. That's me letting down my whole team.

Each of our roads on this journey is unique. Some are winding, some straighter. Some have too many bumps, whereas the lucky ones among us have just enough bumps to learn from. A roadmap provides only the direction. It's an aid to help you navigate. This *Roadmap* was written to help you think about your options before the ball reaches you.

Acknowledgments

A book doesn't just happen. Rather, it's a product of a team effort. To those on my team, I offer my sincere gratitude.

My team at John Wiley & Sons started with my dear friend Debby Englander who is, frankly, the best in the business. Special thanks also goes to a smart and dedicated editor, Emilie Herman; Tula Batanchiev, who shepherded the book; production editor Melissa Lopez; Danny Vasquez; and to Cape Cod Compositors.

Jodi Lipson, director of the AARP Books Division, led the AARP team. She was supportive throughout the process and had great insights. She also brought in talented teammates: Heather Nawrocki, director of AARP Media Promotions; Anne Masters, art director; Scott A. Davis, creative director; Susan O'Brian, researcher; and Eli Meir Kaplan, photographer. AARP staff experts who reviewed the book included Elizabeth Bradley, Mary Liz Burns, Betsy Carpenter, Lauren Grider, Sally Hurme, Enid Kassner, Gary Koenig, Leslie Nettleford, Michael Schuster, Alison Shelton, Yolanda Taylor, Lori Trawinski, Mikki Waid, and Lisa Yagoda.

Thanks also go to elder law attorneys Gary Mazart and Crystal C. West and to financial adviser Bill Gillett.

A huge thanks goes to all the friends, relatives, and colleagues I interviewed, and especially to those who allowed me to tell their stories. All of them were open and honest with me, sharing their concerns and providing me with their great insight. They were the heart and soul of the team.

Finally, to Gail Sheehy, I offer my special thanks for the time and expertise she invested in writing the foreword and for providing the inspiration for the book.

About the Author

Bart Astor is a recognized expert in life's transitions and eldercare. His unexpected personal journey led him to write his book *Baby Boomer's Guide to Caring for Aging Parents,* now in its second printing and critically regarded as one of today's must-have health-care resources. Astor has written 11 other books as well as web content on eldercare, student financial aid, college admission, insurance, buying a home, and corporate social responsibility. He was also the publisher and founder of the *College Planning Quarterly.* He has appeared on numerous TV and radio shows, including ABC's *Good Morning America,* PBS's *Marketplace,* and Ric Edelman's *The Truth About Money.*

Astor served as Director of Financial Aid at several colleges and universities and represented the National Association of State Student Grant and Aid Programs in Washington, DC. He has a Bachelor of Arts from Carnegie Mellon University and a Master's of Public Administration degree from San Jose State University. Astor lives in Reston, Virginia, with his wife, Kathie Little-Astor, and their two border collies, Bailey and Skye. Follow him on Twitter at #BartAstor.

Visit: www.BartAstor.com.

Index

Index

eligibility requirements for, 56–57

Medicare, 31, 53–56, 61–62, 73
medicine and, 38
Part A, 54
Part B, 54–55
Part C, 55
Part D, 55–56

Medications, 26. *See also* Prescriptions
depression and, 45

Medicine, 36–39
addiction of, 37
buying, 38–39
coordinating, 37
cost of, 37
dosage of, 39
management of, 37
ongoing, 39
prescriptions and, 37–38
side effects of, 37

Medigap, 56, 61

Memory impairment, 27–28
coping with, 28–29

Money, 71–94. *See also* Assets; Finances
access to, 143–146
affinity cards and, 93
assessing whether you have enough, 84–86
credit and, 93
credit cards and, 93
evaluating Social Security, 73–78
financial advice, 72–73
fixed and variable expenses, 96–98
gifts, 91–92

home as asset, 88–90
making it last, 93–94
other sources of funds, 90–92
planning for later years, 79–84
taking required minimum withdrawals, 87
traveling and, 124
viatical settlements, 92

MOOCs. *See* Massive Open Online courses

Mortgage, reverse, 89–90

Moving, 163–168
distance and, 165–166
location, 164–165
overview, 163–164
real estate agents and, 165
stress and, 164
type of housing, 167–168

N

Nearsightedness, 31
Networking, 113
Notary publics, 132
Nursing homes, 57, 58, 59

O

OLLI. *See* Osher Lifelong Learning Institutes
Osher Lifelong Learning Institutes (OLLI), 118

P

Partner. *See also* Remarriage
employment and, 104–106
heirs and, 151–152
life, 10–11
remarriage, 186–189

Index

W
Walking, 23–24
Well-being, 21–49. *See also*
  Bucket list; Quality of life
  appetite, 26
  choosing doctors, 39–43
  dental health, 29–31
  depression and, 43–46
  eating habits, 25–27
  exercise and, 22–25
  grief and, 193
  hearing, 32–36
  incapacity, 145–146
  keeping fit and young at
    heart, 22–27

medicine and, 36–39
overview, 21
pets and, 196
senior moments, 27–29
temperature and, 47–48
transitioning from full-time
  work, 95–106
vision, 31–32
Wills. *See* Ethical wills; Last will
  and testament
Women, single, living abroad
  and, 176
Working out, 24–25
Writing, 126–127

If you enjoyed this book, you may also like these:

New American Diet (AARP)
by John Whyte, MD
ISBN: 9781118185117

Social Security For
Dummies (AARP)
by Jonathan Peterson
ISBN: 9781118205730

The Single Woman's Guide
to Retirement (AARP),
by Jan Cullinane
ISBN: 9781118229507

Great Jobs for Everyone
50+ (AARP),
by Kerry Hannon
ISBN: 9781118203682